Praise for UX Research

"It's crucial that product development teams tap into their empathy to deliver better experiences for their customers. UX Research provides practical, feet-on-the-ground guidance for conducting research to inform product strategy and design efforts in any organization."

PETER MERHOLZ—DESIGN AND PRODUCT EXECUTIVE

"Research is rigor. It's the difference between designing for real humans and just having an opinion. This book will tell you what you need to know about research from the earliest considerations through to the analysis and implementation. It will help you choose the right method and tell you how to execute with lots of great anecdotal information you can only get from people who've done the work. It's also a great reference piece, you'll be marking the pages and using it over and over."

ADAM POLANSKY—UX STRATEGIST

"This is the book that I wish we would have written if we would have turned each chapter of A Project Guide to UX Design into its own book. Brad and David take a topic that is frequently not considered as complex and complicated as it is, and they spell it out clearly for you. Even better, they not only tell you what to do, they tell you what not to do based upon their own research and experiences. If you want to get started in research, you need to get your start with this book."

RUSS UNGER—DESIGN LEADER, COAUTHOR OF
A PROJECT GUIDE TO UX DESIGN,
DESIGNING THE CONVERSATION,
AND *SPEAKER CAMP*

"Finally, a book that delves deep into research methods for UX work! Our field needs a book with this level of rigor and detail. Brad and David have written the essential guide to planning, conducting, and evaluating UX research. I suggest you buy a few copies because I guarantee this book will get stolen off your desk."

KAREN MCGRANE—MANAGING PARTNER,

BOND ART + SCIENCE

"Observation is the door to empathy. UX Research offers practical steps to help you better understand the people you serve, and make better product and business decisions as a result. This is the most comprehensive guide to research I've seen in such an accessible format."

WHITNEY HESS—EMPATHY COACH

"This is a soup-to-nuts guide to get the insights you need to make your project a success. The authors have thought of all the little details to make what seems like a simple task go smoothly, and it's sprinkled with field-tested insights from expert practitioners. Whatever the question was that brought you to this book, you'll find the answers between these covers."

NASIR BARDAY—PRINCIPAL USER EXPERIENCE ARCHITECT,

TANDEMSEVEN, INC.

"Practical, right-sized experience research is a vastly undervalued part of product management and design. That's why UX Research is a welcome and valuable tool. The authors have assembled a rich overview—detailed enough to convey the essentials, but compact and straightforward enough for non-specialists. This is a great resource I look forward to sharing with my business partners and UX peers."

ANDREW HINTON—AUTHOR OF *UNDERSTANDING CONTEXT*

"Whether you are a university student or a well-seasoned design practitioner, UX Research *is a remarkable one-stop shop for understanding the world of user experience research. Brad Nunnally and David Farkas do an exceptional job combining theory, practical takeaways, and anecdotal information from other remarkable practitioners to provide a comprehensive must-have book for every designer."*

**DIEGO PULIDO—VP UX DESIGN LEAD,
JP MORGAN CHASE**

"This is the book I wish I had when I started doing my own research. It distills years of insights, tips, and best practices collected and curated by two seasoned experts in the field. If you're interested in doing your own research—whether you've done it before or not—you can learn everything either by spending years going through trial and error, or by reading this book and knowing that you're on the right track, doing quality work, and having an impact on your projects, products, and business."

DONNA LICHAW—AUTHOR OF *THE USER'S JOURNEY*

UX Research

Practical Techniques for
Designing Better Products

Brad Nunnally and David Farkas

Beijing · Boston · Farnham · Sebastopol · Tokyo

UX Research

by Brad Nunnally and David Farkas

Copyright © 2017 Brad Nunnally and David Farkas. All rights reserved.

Printed in the United States of America.

Published by O'Reilly Media, Inc., 1005 Gravenstein Highway North, Sebastopol, CA 95472.

Development Editor: Angela Rufino

Acquisitions Editor: Nicolas Lombardi

Production Editor: Colleen Cole

Copyeditor: Rachel Monaghan

Proofreader: Jasmine Kwityn

Indexer: Lucie Haskins

Interior Designer: David Futato

Cover Designer: Karen Montgomery

Illustrator: Rebecca Demarest

November 2016: First Edition

Revision History for the First Edition
2016-11-04: First Release

See *http://www.oreilly.com/catalog/errata.csp?isbn=0636920048336* for release details.

978-1-491-95129-3

[LSI]

[contents]

[*Foreword*]

IN THE LATE 1940s, a psychology professor named Roger Barker ran a lengthy contextual research project in the small Kansas town of Oskaloosa. For over 25 years, researchers observed and logged the activities of the town's 725 residents. The notion of doing research about everyday people's behavior in context (rather than in a laboratory) was radical at the time. In exhaustive detail, Barker documented ordinary activities throughout the day. Because it was a new approach to studying people, it wasn't obvious how this data would lead to any insight. And while the results of Barker's work were considered significant, there was an element of notoriety simply because of the volume of banal data he captured. I'm obviously oversimplifying terribly here, but consider that Barker may represent an era of academic research that privileged data over questions.

In product design today, we start with questions. Those questions may include a hypothesis, an assumption, or a set of missing information, but for the most part we set out to conduct research because there's something that we need to know in order to build or improve a product, tool, service, or the like. And with practice, we can learn to do a pretty reasonable job of answering the questions we start with. But a vital outcome of research (not just the data that is gathered but the experiences we have in gathering it) is learning about what we didn't know that we didn't know. The most important insights often lie beyond the questions that we started with. Answering this initial set of questions is necessary, but often insufficient in order to impact our products in a meaningful way.

But to pull off this level of research requires a certain level of skill. Research is seemingly just getting people to answer your questions and sneakily implies a low barrier to entry for new researchers. An untrained surgeon acting from instinct would probably not do well ("it's just cutting into people, right?"), but at least they would realize that. Research lures the unconsciously incompetent.

With practice, reflection, mentorship, and training (look at what you are holding in your hands), we can make progress. And yet research continues to challenge us. On a personal level, we have to be patient, be present, be curious, be prepared to set our assumptions aside. Professionally, we have to not only uncover insights, but also be on schedule and within budget, work to the pace that our audience defines, and create learning-ready moments to drive the internalization of information.

These professional challenges only exacerbate the personal challenges. When the team wants to constrain the question, the answer, and the approach, how can you possibly go out in the field and act patiently? When the team is excited (an emotion that sometimes presents as impatience), how can you possibly take the time to plan and to reflect? Yet the people (like you) that lean into this work know at an implicit level that this is how you get to the good stuff.

Doing research this way is unabashedly human. Research is about us as people and how we are with other people, which is fundamental to how we spend our time on earth. People learning research skills report on how it gives them a different handle on other interactions in their lives, with coworkers, with friends, and with loved ones. If you're someone who knows and loves research, you might sometimes feel that research is about, well, just everything. And that everything leads us back to thinking about research. And while no book of finite size can be about everything, there's a comprehensiveness here that reminds us how important this broad, inclusive view is.

Throughout this book you'll find exercises that connect the tasks of research with the act of being in the world. This is a great strategy for building confidence. The book offers several ways to learn research through everyday practices. As a bonus, you'll probably find that the research skills you learn can be applied to everyday situations. You'll also see a good number of templates and sample tools. You can benefit from their experience and the work they've put in to pull it all together.

David and Brad appropriately frame the work of research as rooted in the context of making stuff (or if you prefer, "product design"). Unlike Roger Barker, we've got to ship something as part of this process. The more wide-eyed we are in our approach to research, the easier it is to lose sight of that ultimate objective.

David and Brad also take care in explaining the details required at various stages of the research process, articulating clearly what to do and what not to do. Many times we take that sort of thing for granted. One might be tempted to dismiss the detailed guidance as "obvious," but the tactics of research require us to challenge some of our default behaviors. What's obvious to one isn't obvious to another.

From the novice to the seasoned, research at its core is challenging. This book acknowledges that, and through the tools here you can recognize and manage those challenges—and ultimately improve how you address them. Research includes planning, organizing, managing, and leading. As readers of this book (that's you!) become better researchers, you will take on more of those facets. Wherever you are in your development, this book is the way to keep moving forward.

—STEVE PORTIGAL

[*Preface*]

Assumptions This Book Makes

This book is written for the user experience practitioners, designers, and managers being asked to conduct product research. It is written for the individuals who will be doing the research and need a quick reference on the rationale and process, as well as for the managers who are looking for a common language to discuss and ultimately sell research.

There is often mystery around product research, and an assumption that you need to be a Zen master of research methods to gather insights. This book intends to pull back the curtain on that assumption. Anyone can conduct product research. While nothing replaces practice and experience, those who read this book will be armed with a common language and set of tools to conduct research in an informed and productive manner.

Contents of This Book

This book is organized into four parts. Within each chapter, we provide the perspective of a professional working in the industry and we close with a short exercise (5–15 minutes) to practice the ideas presented in the book. We will reference documents and artifacts, and our companion website aims to provide sample templates of many of these documents for your use.

Part I, Introduction (Chapter 1)
Offers a brief introduction to UX research by exploring where research has come from and the various fields that impact our work.

Part II, Planning and Preparation (Chapters 2–7)

Shifts to understanding the breadth of research available to practitioners. Chapter 2 defines the most basic element of any research initiative: a good question. After defining what makes a good question, we look at the two types of research in detail. Chapters 3 and 4 introduce quantitative and qualitative research methods, respectively. Having distinguished between the two methods, we then discuss how you might choose the appropriate one in Chapter 5. Next, Chapter 6 explores the logistics and often-overlooked details of coordinating a research session; this includes timing, technology, and maintaining your own well-being. Chapter 7 closes Part II by discussing how you recruit participants to conduct research with.

Part III, Facilitating Research (Chapters 8–12)

Having clearly outlined the planning and preparation phase in the previous chapters, this part moves on to the making and doing phase. Chapter 8 looks at the fundamental skills needed to make research happen. This addresses many other logistics not covered in Chapter 7, including honorariums, practicing your session, and maintaining a professional approach to research. Chapter 9 focuses on the most important part of any research: your first impression, or warm-up. As research takes a lot of practice and often changes as it happens, Chapter 10 explores improvisational acting techniques as a tool to support and inform our research practice. Still, no amount of preparation, planning, and hard skills can prepare you for all aspects of research. The human element is the greatest challenge, so Chapter 11 looks at some human variables to be aware of. We close Part III with Chapter 12, which discusses debrief sessions and the importance of and approaches to keeping your team and business stakeholders informed.

Part IV, Analysis and Reporting (Chapters 13–15)

Looks at how your hard-earned research can be analyzed, organized, and ultimately communicated. The first step is to analyze your findings, and Chapter 13 provides common tools and approaches to taking raw data and uncovering meaning. Chapter 14 takes these unformed insights and provides a framework and structure for communicating your findings. We close the book with Chapter 15, which looks at the value of research throughout a product's lifecycle and highlights additional resources and opportunities for growth.

O'Reilly Safari

Safari (formerly Safari Books Online) is a membership-based training and reference platform for enterprise, government, educators, and individuals.

Members have access to thousands of books, training videos, Learning Paths, interactive tutorials, and curated playlists from over 250 publishers, including O'Reilly Media, Harvard Business Review, Prentice Hall Professional, Addison-Wesley Professional, Microsoft Press, Sams, Que, Peachpit Press, Adobe, Focal Press, Cisco Press, John Wiley & Sons, Syngress, Morgan Kaufmann, IBM Redbooks, Packt, Adobe Press, FT Press, Apress, Manning, New Riders, McGraw-Hill, Jones & Bartlett, and Course Technology, among others.

For more information, please visit *http://oreilly.com/safari*.

How to Contact Us

Please address comments and questions concerning this book to the publisher:

O'Reilly Media, Inc.
1005 Gravenstein Highway North
Sebastopol, CA 95472
800-998-9938 (in the United States or Canada)
707-829-0515 (international or local)
707-829-0104 (fax)

We have a web page for this book, where we list errata, examples, and any additional information. You can access this page at:

http://bit.ly/ux-research-orm

To comment or ask technical questions about this book, send email to:

bookquestions@oreilly.com

For more information about our books, courses, conferences, and news, see our website at *http://www.oreilly.com*.

Find us on Facebook: *http://facebook.com/oreilly*

Follow us on Twitter: *http://twitter.com/oreillymedia*

Watch us on YouTube: *http://www.youtube.com/oreillymedia*

Acknowledgments

FROM BRAD

It's never easy writing a book, but doing so with a great partner like David Farkas has made the process both pleasant and seamless. He has been a wonderful partner throughout this endeavor, and this book wouldn't be in your hands without him.

There are three other people I owe the world to: my loving wife Kim, my son Tristan, and my daughter Payton. I am blessed to have their presence and their support in my life. My wife is truly a superhero for all the support she's given me during the writing of this book and for shouldering way too many bedtimes solo. My children have been that random distraction and laugh when I needed it the most while bogged down with the latest chapter.

I owe everything to my family, especially my mother and father for showing me the importance of the written word by teaching me the wonders available to me through the act of reading. This debt extends to my in-laws, who have always supported my endeavors and offered guidance when I needed it the most. Also, thank you to my sister and brother, who are always there for me when I need them.

A special note of thanks goes out to Olivia Saldaña for taking time out of her life to help us with this book by producing the lovely illustrations you'll find throughout, Tom Greever for suggesting that this was a book we could write, and Russ Unger and Dan Willis for showing me how to write a book in the first place without losing my mind.

I am grateful to my many friends and professional peers who've provided me with advice and mentorship over the years: Diego Pulido, Eduardo Ortiz, Chris Avore, Jared Spool, Lou Rosenfeld, Christina Wodtke, Lis Huburt, Andrea Mignolo, Andrew Hinton, Carol Righi, Dana Chisnell, and many more who have chatted with me over drinks while sharing ideas and letting my voice be heard. My life would not be where it is without so many great people being part of it. And finally, my career would not be what it is without the help of both Whitney Hess and Jonathan "Yoni" Knoll—these two took a clueless Midwesterner coming to New York City for the first time and introduced me to a world of wonderful people, ideas, and challenges.

FROM DAVID

First and foremost, I want to thank my parents for supporting me in everything I do and even encouraging me to literally draw on the walls. And many thanks to my grandparents, my brother Ben, sister Lisa, and niece Hannah, for always being there and giving me reason to smile. And of course a special thanks to my coauthor Brad for taking me on this amazing ride with him.

While I've had many teachers and mentors over the years, I want to thank four in particular: Jim Hunter and Tom Wyroba, my high school art teachers from New World School of the Arts for taking a chance on me (this book stands in honor of your memory), and Mark Mentzer and Mark Baskinger of Carnegie Mellon University for fostering an environment to ask the right (and wrong) questions.

I wouldn't have completed this project without the support of my colleagues at EPAM and their willingness to pose for numerous photos. And to everyone else I have collaborated with, from other organizations to the group of knucklehead practitioners across the map that I call my friends, thank you. And thank you to the local PhillyCHI community and the broader community as a whole, who have given me advice and support over the years. This includes, but certainly is not limited to, Eduardo Ortiz, Debra Levin Gelman, Jonathan "Yoni" Knoll, Tracy Kroop, Scott Weidman, Russ Unger, Jamie Thomson, Diego Pulido, Whitney Hess, Jared Spool, Lou Rosenfeld, Chris Avore, Amy Silvers, John Yuda, Ian Smiles, Abby Covert, and Fred Beecher. Lastly, to my friends and family from home, may this book provide some insight as to what it is I actually do for a living.

FROM US BOTH

We must first thank Angela Rufino and Nick Lombardi for inviting us to join the O'Reilly family. Our many thanks to Steve Portigal for the gracious foreword and to Olivia Saldaña for rendering our chicken scratch illustrations beautifully.

For providing an editing eye to our words, thank you to Lis Hubert, Dan Brown, and Adriana De La Cuadra.

To all those who contributed their voice, a huge thank you: Amber Case, Colin MacArthur, Matthew Wakemen, Sara Yachter-Boettcher, Kevin Richardson, Ron Strawbridge, Jeremy Canfield, Emma Lawler, Lis Hubert, Adam Polansky, Kyle Soucy, Bibiana Nunes, Abby Covert, Dan Brown, and Ofer Deshe.

And thanks to those who helped contribute themselves or their work for reproduction in the book: Jamie Thompson, Andy Scott, Eduardo Ortiz, Russ Unger, Josh Soldiers, Jesse Szygiel, Shannon Patrick, Molly Brennan, Kate Carney, Crystal Irvin, Sarah Etter, Kyle Bruley, and Rebecca Deery.

And thank you, our readers, for choosing to spend your time reading our thoughts on research. We hope you enjoy.

[Part I]

Introduction

THIS PART OF THE BOOK, comprising Chapter 1, offers a brief introduction to UX research by exploring where research has come from and the various fields that impact our work.

[1]

The History of Research

If we knew what it was we were doing, it would not be called research, would it?
—ALBERT EINSTEIN

Before jumping into the methods and approaches of research, it is important to spend some time discussing where research started and its evolution into the processes and methodologies that user experience (UX) practitioners use today. Over the next few pages, we will offer a brief introduction to the history of research in manufacturing, web, and product design. We will compare the rigor of research in academic settings with the streamlined and often-accelerated research found in product design. If you already feel comfortable with the history of research, or are eager to get directly into the making, feel free to jump to Chapter 2.

Research in Manufacturing

Some could argue that product development dates back to the earliest cavemen and their stone tools. If we accept this argument, product research existed long before the title "user experience professional." Research existed before the Web and digital age, before the day of disruptors and crowdsourcing, and before conversations about getting seats at the proverbial table. For this discussion we will look at the turn of the 20th century and the "second industrial revolution" as the beginning of product design and research. It was then that advances in manufacturing and mass production allowed improvements in efficiency and utility to be explored in a scalable and measurable manner.

INDUSTRIAL ENGINEERING

According to the Institute of Industrial Engineers, industrial engineering is "concerned with the design, improvement and installation of integrated systems of people, materials, information, equipment and energy."[1] If this sounds similar to the work of user experience designers, it's because we also focus on the design and improvement of systems. In our work, a system is more than just a website. Systems include customer-facing experience, code, the backend systems, content management systems (CMSs), customer relationship managers (CRMs), and a wide range of physical and digital tools. Just because our systems are integrated with circuit boards and screens doesn't reduce the challenge.

One of the earliest industrial engineers was Frank Gilbreth—the same Frank Gilbreth who wrote *Cheaper by the Dozen*. His contribution to product design and research focused on motion study. Gilbreth believed that by understanding how people moved in space we could design and engineer more efficient systems.

Gilbreth's earliest work focused on how bricklayers lay stonework at construction sites. By recording multiple bricklayers and watching the playback, Gilbreth was able to measure and understand the impact of different postures and motions on work efficiency. He was then able to standardize motions to improve worker productivity overall. The University of Chicago offers sample videos of Gilbreth's early studies,[2] and Figure 1-1 illustrates how these videos captured motion using light and extended exposure.

Gilbreth took his work beyond construction and contracted with the government on the manufacturing of small arms. The study of micro interactions in the physical space and the layout of machines in a workspace had a large impact on worker efficiency and the evolution of modern assembly lines. These improvements were not made based on blind guesses and happenstance, but by Gilbreth's scientific and measured

---

1 About IISE: *https://www.iienet2.org/details.aspx?id=282*

2 Motion Pictures in the Human Sciences, "The Original Films of Frank Gilbreth" (*https://lucian.uchicago.edu/blogs/sciencefilm/human-sciences-on-film/human-movement-3/frank-gilbreth-films*).

approach to improving the lives and efficiency of employees. This is very similar to how we as practitioners seek to improve efficiency and ease the work for our clients and customers.

FIGURE 1-1

Gilbreth's motion studies captured the movement of hands, arms, and head by tracking light sensors through delayed camera exposure

AUTOMOBILES

Speaking of assembly lines, Henry Ford is often credited with introducing the modern assembly line. Rather than have workers build a product in a set location, moving machinery to and from the work in progress, the assembly line moves the product being built through a shop to different specialized stations. The employees themselves focus on specific tasks and have their tools available within arm's reach.

While it would be easy to stop here and say automobiles and assembly lines capture the ideal of product research by increasing efficiency through iterative measurements and improvements, research did not stop with Ford. Today's car manufacturers are still looking for new ways to improve the production process. The research doesn't need to be all white lab coats and motion studies, either.

General Motors, for instance, in teaming with Toyota, has explored new ways of supporting employee suggestions and modifications to workflow. This may be the placement of a drill in a workbench or adjusting the speed at which a part moves through the factory to allow for optimal attention and accuracy. After all, who knows the challenges of a task better than those completing them? By creating an environment that rewards innovation and trying new methods, the automobile industry continues to innovate both processes and technique. NPR's *This American Life* has a great episode from 2015 on this process that we highly recommend you listen to (*http://www.thisamericanlife.org/radio-archives/episode/561/nummi-2015*).

Human Factors

The manufacturing age introduced improvements in factories and large-scale machinery as the world became digital with integrated circuits and microchips. *Human factors* is a term often synonymous with the digital age, but this field of study existed before the computer and the microchip. While there are many early examples of human factors, one of our favorites is the evolution of the Golden Triangle as it is referenced in kitchen design.

THE GOLDEN TRIANGLE

The *Golden Triangle* is the term ascribed to the position of the sink, oven, and refrigerator in a modern kitchen. Through motion studies as well as the study of human physiology, researchers understood that the most efficient layout for a kitchen loosely follows this triangular pattern (Figure 1-2).

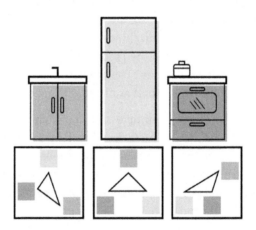

FIGURE 1-2

Three common ways to establish the golden triangle in the kitchen based on different layouts. Each shows the ideal relative placement of the refrigerator, stove, and sink.

What fascinates us about the Golden Triangle is that it shows intent to improve an everyday behavior for consumers. This is a remarkably different approach than focusing on engineering and manufacturing as areas to improve efficiency. While some might say a more efficient kitchen leads to cooking more and more home-related purchases, we like to take commerce out of the focus and realize that research was happening to improve individuals' lives on a personal level.

Analytics and Lab Coats

As the 20th century continued and the digital age took off, new methods and techniques for evaluating design and behavior needed to be considered. Utility was no longer limited to the distance from the sink to the stove, or the distance a drill needs to move to assemble the chassis of a car. IBM and Xerox PARC are often credited with the growth of the human–computer interaction (HCI) field, and rightly so. These companies introduced design paradigms such as color-coding office printer parts for streamlined maintenance and access. And it was in those offices that Douglas Engelbart invented the first computer mouse. These revolutions came with adjustments in approach to usability and success. One popular method addresses the *goals, operators, methods, and selection* rules, or GOMS.

GOMS

UX practitioners love and often overuse acronyms. In the case of GOMS, this made-up word is for the practical reason of brevity. Goals, operators, methods, and selection rules measure the intent and process of a system. Conveniently, this approach can apply to both physical and digital spaces.

GOMS defined

Let's define the four pillars of GOMS in more detail. Being academically focused terms, these are not phrases heard around the office, though their meaning and implications are present in everything we do. By defining these pillars together we can understand how they relate to research tasks and opportunities.

Goals asks the question "What do you want to do?" The answer might be as simple as opening a window on a computer, making a photocopy, or setting the temperature of the thermostat in your home. It is important to keep in mind that certain goals can be timeless, though the method of achieving them changes. For example, while adjusting the temperature of a home once meant opening a window or turning on a furnace, in recent years it's become as simple as setting a thermostat or enabling a smart home device (Figure 1-3). Looking beyond the definition of the task, goals incorporate mental awareness and preparation. This pillar questions participants' frame of mind and clarifies what supporting information might be needed to be successful not just in the moment but also throughout a task.

FIGURE 1-3
Nest thermostat in a typical home environment

Operators seeks to understand "What tools do you have as a person to get the job done?" Whereas the focus of goals is intent, operators help identify the cognitive hurdles of a task. How might my hands, eyes, and other senses be used to complete a task? How might physical limitations impact what I want to do? A common phrase heard around workshops is "If all you have is a hammer, every problem looks like a nail." Asking what tools we have available—be it our fingers, eyes, voice, or gestures—is important in understanding how we engage with the world around us. With ubiquitous computing, wearables, and the sharing economy, engagement with a product goes beyond what we can point to and see immediately in front of us. How do height and other physical differences impact task completion? How might age impact our perception and understanding of an environment?

Methods looks at "How can the tools, or operators, be used to complete the task?" If you are shopping for a new computer you are immediately asked to choose different configurations—processor speed and hard drive, monitor size, and keyboard preference. As designers we are faced with similar questions. Is a system built with toggles, switches, or more dynamic screens and systems? What are the different interactions that need to be supported so the user can accomplish their goals?

Selection rules, the final pillar of GOMS, measures the various options an interface or product offers to assist users in accomplishing their goals. A light switch, for instance, has two states, on and off, and two rules, turn something on or off. An interface may have hundreds or thousands of rules, especially something like Adobe Illustrator, where the toolbar alone provides nearly limitless options (Figure 1-4).

FIGURE 1-4

Adobe Illustrator's toolbar illustrates the wide variety of selection rules available in a single digital product

GOMS in practice: Keystroke-Level Modeling

GOMS are a fascinating tool to understand the makeup of a product. Alone they are more a descriptor and less a measurement. Keystroke-Level Modeling (KLM) is the most common application of GOMS in the digital space.

At its simplest, KLM is the mathematical study of a tool's efficiency. Intended to measure completion tasks for expert users, KLM could also be defined as motion study for digital products.

KLM studies measure the time it takes to complete a micro interaction, such as clicking a mouse or pressing a key. Using Fitts's law, a mathematical equation that determines task time by calculating the size of targets and their distance from one another, KLM can provide an estimate for task completion for various interfaces (Figure 1-5). By changing the size and position of different elements on a screen, KLM studies can measure the efficiency of different solutions.

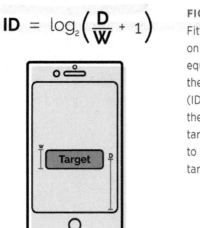

$$ID = \log_2\left(\frac{D}{W} + 1\right)$$

FIGURE 1-5

Fitts's law is based on the mathematical equation that computes the Index of Difficulty (ID) by measuring the distance between targets (D) compared to the size of the targets (W)

While many tools exist to support KLM measures, they are limited to digital artifacts. CogTool is one product developed by Bonnie John of IBM Research and formerly of Carnegie Mellon University's Human–Computer Interaction Institute. CogTool provides a simple interface to set up automated scripts to measure the efficiency of different designs. If you are interested in this technique, we highly suggest exploring the CogTool website (*http://cogtool.com*) and GitHub repo (*https://github.com/cogtool*) for more information.

It is important to note that while GOMS are very informative regarding task completion time, they are limited primarily to digital products. While they ask questions about cognitive processing, they are limited in their understanding of accessibility. For instance, colors and color blindness are not measured by GOMS.

Voice from the Streets

Amber Case,
Cyborg Anthropologist

In a few words, describe your job.

I'm known as a cyborg anthropologist, a field of study that looks at how technology affects culture, and I recently finished a book on nonintrusive interactions called *Calm Technology* (O'Reilly).

As someone with a background in the sciences, how do research methods apply to your work?

I don't have a standard "day in the life." Mostly I am doing qualitative research. My research comes from traveling, observing, and speaking with people about how they use hardware and software.

1. **Marinate.**

   When I'm first tasked to figure out how to design or improve a product, I saturate myself in it completely. The first thing I do is look at the history of that product. Where did it come from? What was it inspired by? What came before it? What analog idea did it improve on or replace? I try to find the motivations for why something needs to exist. This can give me some clues on where a design might go in the future and how to help it get there. I also want to see how other people have tried to solve the problem. I don't like to deviate too far from what's out there when I do design work. I simply want to remove unnecessary interactions. As I research, I save screenshots to my filesystem and jot down quick vignettes. Depending on the timeframe, this can take anywhere from a couple of days to a couple of weeks.

2. **Socialize.**

   The next step is to observe people using the product. I want to see where they get frustrated, where they are enthralled, and where they are disgusted. I am looking for emotional states, friction, and stories. I usually jot these down in the Notepad app on my phone as well as take videos of the interactions on my phone. For instance, if I'm doing research on vehicles I'll take rides with people and watch them using the dashboard of a car. I'll rent a car myself and focus on specific elements of the interaction. The most important thing I am trying to gather here are stories, as they give me perspectives on experience. I know when I'm nearing the completion of this stage when I start to get a lot of repeated experiences and personal stories. Then I know it is time to compile the vignettes and research together.

3. **Digest.**

The next stage is digestion—I take all of the stories and notes I have and compress them into similar stories. This is where I get my user stories. They have to be real experiences from the real world. I have to have experienced them with someone, or at least get as close as I can to the experiences. When I'm testing a product, I use those perspectives to see if it works. I try to put on as many perspectives as I can. When I design or redesign a product I want to look at it through many eyes, not just my own.

4. **Design.**

At this point I create a document or slideshow with design recommendations. This involves diagrams, screenshots, and short vignettes from the ethnographic research I completed previously. I show the experiences people have with the current product or the current situation and how a specific design can improve those interactions. For a complex product, I may call technical support and ask about their most common troubleshooting calls. Those are the first sites of improvement. It is important to create products that are easy to support as well as use. Ideally a product shouldn't need any customer support at all.

If I'm designing alone I will create mockups and wireframes for the entire system. If I am designing with a team I'll work with software engineers and UX designers in the same room. I want what is implemented on the frontend to be easy to implement on the backend as well. Again, I'm into the least amount of design to get something to work very well. Each new feature adds complexity to software development, UX testing, and support. It's better to let the community lead and build a strong channel for communication as the product advances. I often suggest hiring the most die-hard users, or having the product team listen to support requests to see how the product is used. I enjoy companies like Airbnb, as they require their employees to book lodging during travel on the Airbnb site itself. It's easier to detect issues if everyone uses the software.

Computers, the Web, and Today

In today's world, you can't turn your head without seeing a product or service that is designed. Everything from the apps and form factor of your phone to smart thermostats and the integrated advertisements you see when shopping has a team of designers and researchers evaluating how to best attract our attention (Figure 1-6).

FIGURE 1-6
Apple Developer SDK

This wasn't always the case. Early technology was made to be utilitarian. The first word processor, WordStar, was meant to imitate a typewriter. It displayed green or white text on a black screen (Figure 1-7). It wasn't until years later that word processors were made to render black text on a white screen, imitating paper. And still later iterations introduced toolbars and formatting options.

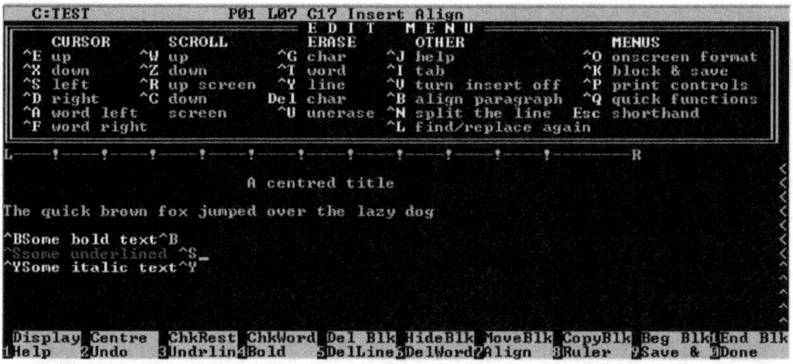

FIGURE 1-7

WordStar 3.0, launched in 1982 (image source: *https://en.wikipedia.org/w/index.php?curid=37398368*)

Traditional command-line services were ultimately replaced by graphical user interfaces (GUIs). And the use of windows, icons, menus, and pointers became common.

Today, a sleek interface is not enough. Designers must provide a compelling service to their customers. In this way, we have come full circle to product research and design. Where in the 1990s it was enough to be utilitarian, services now must also strike on an emotional level. Where in the early 2000s a web presence was a distinguishing factor, services must now be integrated. Our phones are smarter, our homes online, and our cars (almost) self-driving. How do data, desires, and motivations impact the evolution of these services? How do we better understand human motivations and needs?

The answer is research. Research allows product teams to get out of their own heads and see the world as it is and design around that understanding.

While the rest of this book will look at the practical application of various research methods, we will close this first chapter by highlighting where research finds its historical roots.

Field Research Takes Root

What began at IBM and Xerox PARC has continued to grow for decades at academic departments in the form of human–computer interaction coursework. While their title might be newer as a specific career path, UX practitioners have backgrounds in a wide range of fields.

This offers our industry a unique perspective. Rather than thousands of people with the same professional upbringing and perspective, our mosaic of backgrounds arms UX designers, researchers, and developers with the skills to take on digital interfaces, physical products, and the convergence of the two in everyday life. The inclusive nature of our practice allows teams and products to evolve, rather than stagnate, as technologies and needs shift in a fluid marketplace.

THE BACKGROUNDS THAT LED TO UX RESEARCH

While becoming a user experience practitioner is accessible to just about anyone, practitioners commonly come from computer science, psychology, ethnography, library science, and, of course, graphic design, interactive design, or industrial design. Every area of study offers a unique perspective and approach to product design. We highly recommend working in a diverse team made up of folks from different backgrounds, both in terms of education and experience, because it allows you to work more creatively and efficiently.

Those who hail from computer science often have development or IT backgrounds. For anyone looking to build a digital product, these practitioners are paramount to actually making your service. Their understanding of complex systems is a necessity in ensuring the appropriate backend needs are met. Computer science offers a rigor in testing and evaluating code that effectively provides clean, stable, and scalable products.

On the other side of many university campuses, psychology and ethnography majors have found their way to user experience. Many of our qualitative and quantitative research methods (covered in Chapters 3 and 4) are heavily inspired by the work started in these fields. Psychology and ethnography majors make great researchers and are key members of any product research team. Their awareness of and sensitivity to users' emotional and psychological needs ensures a system that is not only efficient but necessary, desired, and responsive to customer needs and limitations.

The library science focus is often disregarded in the digital realm. Looking at the field objectively, library science—which is steeped in classification systems such as Dewey Decimal Classification—is a prime example of taxonomy and structure. Practitioners with library science backgrounds have an affinity for taxonomy, helpful in any product design. As content strategy and information architecture are key aspects of any product strategy, collaborating with team members who have an affinity for this work is critical.

Academia is creating more design programs and producing more and more designers who go into product and digital design. Programs vary from academic focuses to those focusing more on systems and product. In any case, these designers provide an approach to the emotive and human element of a design. They are often able to pivot approaches and needs with fewer technical or procedural constraints, having been trained in an environment to produce results and focus less on statistics.

One important disclaimer is that while we have outlined a small number of backgrounds that UX professionals come from, this is by no means an all-inclusive list. These professions have laid the groundwork for research. Ultimately it is up to the individual designer to adapt methods to their specific needs. This is not intended as a list of education or training one needs to be a product designer or researcher. In fact, many of the best designers, researchers, and managers come from backgrounds so diverse they couldn't all be listed here. One common trait all designers have, though, is the curiosity to ask questions. Next, we will discuss how good research starts with asking the right questions, and what defines a good question.

Parting Thoughts

There is a long-standing history of research. The prevalence of the microchip has shifted focus from pure efficiency to pleasure, desirability, and market differentiation. The rest of this book will outline the framework of various approaches and hurdles in a typical research process. Technology and tools are forever in flux, however, and while we reference specific services, the landscape of tools available is ever growing. We strongly urge you to take the information presented as a baseline for crafting your own practice and evolving methods into your specific workflows.

Part II

Planning and Preparation

EVERY RESEARCHER IS ONLY as good as their research plan. This plan includes all the areas you'll want to explore during your research and the various methods you'll be using. Also, you'll be preparing for recruiting people to perform the research with and determining where and when you'll be holding your sessions. All of these things need to be handled so your research goes smoothly and the information you collect is of good quality and will help your team.

Good Research = Good Questions

> One of the first steps you'll need to master as you start getting into UX research is figuring out what questions you need to answer. In Chapter 2 we will show you how to draft a list of questions and iterate on them so you don't fall into some common pitfalls.

Research Methods: Quantitative and Qualitative

> Chapters 3 and 4 will provide you with a 10,000-foot view of different methods you can use when learning about your users.

Choosing Your Methods

> A vast number of methods are available to you, and part of planning your research is figuring out which are right for you and your team. Chapter 5 will guide you through that process.

Logistics

> There are lots of details that go into conducting any form of research, and they differ based on whether you're doing the research remotely or in person. In Chapter 6 we will cover the logistical items you'll need to plan for so you're set up for success.

Recruitment

> It's kind of hard to do research without researchers. In the final chapter of this part, Chapter 7, we'll cover the various ways for you to recruit people.

[2]

Good Research Starts
with Good Questions

*I don't pretend we have all the answers. But the questions are
certainly worth thinking about.*
—ARTHUR C. CLARKE

Research has always been a part of product development and
design, as showcased by the previous chapter. In today's world,
we are no longer restricted to a single community, population,
or geographical location. Modern products span the globe, sometimes in very unexpected ways. Products may shift in goals
and use over time, and it is through research that the necessary
adjustments are identified.

For teams to conduct meaningful research and collect data that
allows quick iterations, you must start with an idea of what type
of questions you want to ask. Not all questions are created equal,
though, and it is helpful to understand what makes a good question and a good research initiative. If you've ever learned something from another person, you know that asking "good" questions is more craft than science. In this chapter, we discuss this
craft and provide methods you can use to create questions that
help you learn specific topics and remove factors such as personal and unconscious bias. We also provide a short exercise you
can perform to quickly iterate through potential questions to ask
about how someone might want to interact with a product.

Why Are Good Questions So Hard?

Researchers always struggle when it comes to writing down the questions they need to ask their participants. Sure, this gets easier over time and with experience, but the act of writing an interview guide or test plan never gets "easy." At the end of the day, we are all human and we are susceptible to our own weaknesses and limitations.

The deck is stacked against us when you start to consider social, personal, professional, and sometimes logistical factors that can inhibit our ability to have a conversation with someone else. Predicting all these factors before research even starts is no small feat. This in turn makes writing down lines of inquiry that will result in good, useful data seem daunting. But you have to start somewhere and iterate as you learn what questions work and which fall flat. To help you with this, first we need to discuss what role questions fulfill when you're conducting any type of research.

THE ROLE OF QUESTIONS IN RESEARCH

It's hard to conduct research when you don't know what question needs to be answered. Every research effort starts with you needing to know why something happens, what people do in certain circumstances, and how they perform key tasks. To answer these questions, we must find people to talk to and phrase our questions effectively to get to the heart of the matter. Otherwise, we would be making wild guesses and shooting in the dark. While that's often tempting, this degree of freedom leads to failure and your product never seeing the light of day.

HOW GOOD QUESTIONS GO WRONG

We can't tell you how many times we've written down a question and thought, "This is it! This will get us some awesome information from people," only to have it fall flat during a session. This happens to all researchers and it will happen to you. And that's OK! Bad questions can be mitigated through the planning phase if you know what makes a question go bad. The following factors can lead to misinformed or poor research results.

Leading questions

It's easy to get caught up in the excitement of research. This can trick you into asking questions that give participants a clue, or directly point them, to the type of answer you're looking for. These are called leading questions, and they can hinder your research session and the data collected. An example of a leading question would be asking, "How do you use Outlook to communicate your work status?" A better alternative would be "How do you communicate your work status?" The second question allows more responses than leading the participant to describe a specific use of email. Research participants want to be helpful and want to provide value to your team. Since they are primed to help, if you ask a question that implies the type of answer you want, they are more likely to give you that answer, even if it doesn't really apply to them.

Shallow questions

One golden rule of research is never ask yes/no questions. When creating questions for an upcoming research effort, you'll find avoiding these questions is hard. Yes/no questions are harmful because they give participants an easy out. The question "Do you use Yammer for team discussions?" can quickly be answered and dismissed. Participants don't have to think deeply to respond, and they are giving you confirmation that may or may not be useful. A better question is "How do you communicate with your team throughout the day?"

Personal bias

We all have our own beliefs about how products work, or how they should work. These biases can sneak into our questions. The best approach, then, is to remove yourself from the actual research. While strict practice may suggest not conducting the research, we recommend developing questions from the point of view of the product, the customer, or even stakeholders of the product. The less "you" there is in the interview, the better the information that you collect will be. This results in questions more like "Tell me about your experience with your accounting software" than "I know I always struggle with invoices; what challenges do you have with your software?"

Unconscious bias

Our brains make tons of decisions every day, many of which we aren't aware of. These can be influenced by social norms, personal history, past experiences, or expectations. These biases are the hardest to catch. Unconscious biases fail to recognize that others' perception of a situation is not the same as our own. To avoid this, dig deeper no matter how uncomfortable that might make you feel. For instance, gender bias exists within the workplace because most people aren't aware that the bias exists at all. Asking "Where do you guys go to unwind after work?" has implicit gender biases, whereas "Where does your team go after work?" is more neutral.

KNOWING WHEN TO BREAK THE RULES

If you're just starting to build out your research skills, it's important to avoid the aforementioned factors. However, once you get a few studies under your belt, you'll find you can use leading questions and shallow questions in strategic ways. You can even use a participant's personal and unconscious bias to drive to a deeper conversation about how people might use a product.

Leading

These are best used when you suspect the response will be opposite to the hints you provide in your questioning. You can use leading questions to help build trust with a participant and to validate a previous comment they made that maybe wasn't totally clear.

Example: How much do your friends and family appreciate photo albums when you make one for them?

Shallow

When you start a research session, sometimes participants aren't yet comfortable and they need to get used to talking with you and answering your questions. Shallow questions give participants that opportunity and can help ease them into the activity so you can get to the good stuff.

Example: How many times do you log in to Facebook in a day?

Personal bias

There is something to be said about being a good devil's advocate—someone who can take the opposite view in a conversation to spark additional thought or comments. You can use your personal thoughts and opinions to get to deeper conversation by giving the participant something to disagree with.

Example: Do you think the Cubs actually have a chance at the World Series this year?

YEARS OF PRACTICE AND FAILURE TO MASTER

The only way to practice research is by finding people to talk to. The first few studies you run won't be the best, and that's OK! You will learn something after each session, even if every question you ask isn't the best version of that question. The goal is to improve your line of questioning and to find ways to hold a meaningful conversation with someone rather than treat research like a verbal questionnaire.

We have both had our fair share of failing during our years as researchers. In the early days, we asked overly leading questions and missed important areas of discussion because we didn't know what we were looking for. But thanks to mentors providing feedback and guidance, we eventually overcame these failings. We still make some mistakes today, and you will too, but as long as you have a consistent feedback loop in place, you'll continue to improve and eventually master the art of research.

The Basic Structure of a Question

Now that you know what kinds of questions not to ask, let's dive into how to write questions that will get you the information you want. To start, we are going to cover the overall anatomy of a question and different forms questions can take to drive conversations (Figure 2-1).

The setup   Area of inquiry

When you are on a photowalk,   how do you decide what scenes you're going to photograph?

Laddering

How do you determine if a scene has been captured the way you want it?

Segue to next question

Do you do this out in the field or when you get back to your computer?

FIGURE 2-1
The structure of a standard question

THE SETUP

Every question starts with a purpose, or setup. This takes the form of what (description), why (explanation), how (process), when (situation), and where (context). It gives the participant an idea of the type and, more importantly, the length of response you expect out of them.

AREA OF INQUIRY

The area of inquiry is what you want to learn about—for example, how your product impacts or influences someone's life.

LADDERING

Some responses to your questions will have an automatic "Why?" behind them. Asking for a participant to go into more detail or to explain the rationale behind their response is known as laddering, and it's an aspect of a question that helps you get to deeper information and potentially impactful stories. We often joke this is when we get to act like two-year-olds, asking "Why?" to get more information regardless of the answer. The key is to probe enough without being obnoxious, though.

SEGUE TO NEXT QUESTION

The best research sessions are focused conversations between you and a participant. The best way to make an interview or study session feel conversational is to string questions together so the whole session has a beginning, middle, and end. While it is helpful to think about how each question could set up the following question, it is important to keep the discussion fluid, something we will address more in Chapters 9 and 10.

Writing Your Questions

It's time to put pen to paper and generate the list of queries that'll guide your investigations. To begin, our friend Colin MacArthur explains how he creates questions to learn about broad and ambiguous topics.

RELATE BACK TO RESEARCH GOALS

Every question in your interview guide should tie back to why you're doing research in the first place. Remember, every question should target a few key topics or events that relate to your product. If a question won't, or doesn't seem to, provide information that helps you understand these goals, it's vital that you remove it from this line of questioning.

Example: Learn about how people determine which photos to share with family and friends.

> **Bad question:** How do you ensure that you get good composition when you're out taking photos?

Revised question: When you're out taking photos, how do you know a particular shot is worth sharing with people?

OPEN UP ADDITIONAL AREAS OF DISCUSSION

Interviewers make many assumptions when planning the questions and discussion guide order. Some questions are designed to uncover *rabbit holes*, lines of conversation that diverge from the current topic. These are moments where you'll go off-script and improvise the discussion. Rabbit holes are good to explore as long as you're getting good information from them.

Example: Learn why photography matters to the participant.

Unhelpful rabbit hole: My mobile phone just made it so easy to take photos, so I just started taking snapshots throughout my day. *Not much here aside from ease of access and a low barrier of entry to taking photos.*

Helpful rabbit hole: When I was a kid, my neighbor was a photographer and he would let me help out in his darkroom to develop his shots. *Lots of potential stories here, including mentorship and how the participant developed a love for photography.*

PROGRESS THE OVERALL CONVERSATION

We've talked about the importance of research sessions feeling more like conversations than a verbal questionnaire. To ensure this happens, your questions should build upon each other and help guide the participant through topics that have a natural pace. Abrupt changes in conversation can be off-putting and harmful to the information you collect. A sequence of questions may follow this order:

1. What kind of moments do you try to capture when you're out taking photos?

2. What kinds of moments do you treasure or hold dear?

3. When do you decide to print a photo for display?

4. How often do you change the photos you display?

Voice from the Streets

Colin MacArthur,
UX Designer and Researcher

In a few words, describe your job.

I try to figure out how the federal government can better serve its people. Often that starts by conducting interviews with people who do (and don't) use government services.

How do you balance specificity and ambiguity in research?

I spend many of my days planning and conducting interviews with people who use government systems, data, and services.

Figuring out what we want to learn is the easiest part of my day. The hard part is translating our big research questions into good interview questions. We're often trying to answer abstract questions (like "What's hard about interacting with the government?"), but abstract interview questions aren't fruitful. If I ask, "What was hard about your last interaction with the federal government?" I'll get some confused stares, some answers about state governments, and a lot of unelaborated "It was OK."

When we want to get at abstract questions, we give interviewees "handles" that make them more concrete. A common tactic is asking people to think about a recent, significant life change. As they describe what happened, interviewers ask follow-up questions that focus on what we're interested in (interactions with the government). Another approach is giving people specific scenarios and asking them to respond. For example, instead of asking people how they feel about the government collecting health data, we might provide a couple scenarios for discussion.

The challenge is making handles useful, but not leading. If we started questions with very specific questions about particular life events, we could narrow conversations and miss unexpected topics. We try to balance making questions open (and nonleading) with making them easy to answer. That's a hard balance to find, but the best approach is iterative. Repeatedly asking questions to friends and then asking them how hard they were to answer helps me. At the end of the day, I've succeeded when our questions both surface interesting questions and don't put an enormous burden on the interviewee.

How to Use Different Types of Questions

Recall the basic setup of a question: what (description), why (explanation), how (process), when (situation), and where (context). Each of these serves a different function, and you should have a balanced mix planned across the interview guide.

PROCESS

Process-oriented questions are great openers to research sessions, and also useful as topic transitions. They give participants an open area to talk about something they have done and how they did it. You benefit by gaining an impromptu checklist of things you want to learn more about.

Example: How do you design a photo album for a friend or family member?

EXPLANATION

People say the most interesting things, often without knowing why they said them. By requesting that participants explain their comments through the laddering method described earlier, you gain a deeper view into their world. This is where you find valuable information. This could be unexpected and surprising, or it could give you insight into exactly why people do certain things with your product.

Example: Why do you feel that photo albums are still a treasured keepsake in today's world, where more and more photos are digital?

DESCRIPTION

Everyone has his or her own unique way of looking at the world. Research helps you collect these points of view and add them to your own, allowing you to look at product features and roadmaps from a new perspective.

Example: What makes a photo worthy of going into a photo album?

TIME BASED

There are many reasons why a participant might use your product at a particular moment. During an interview, you can ask for explanations about triggers that motivate their picking your product. You can also get insight into how long people spend performing certain actions and how much tolerance they have when something goes wrong.

Example: When do you think photo albums are most appreciated?

FRUSTRATIONS/HURDLES

The motto of a good researcher is "there is no such thing as user error." One thing you'll learn is that many users will blame themselves. These are moments of exploration because you can get to the source of why errors are made and what frustrates users when things don't work out for them.

Example: What do you do when you don't have enough photos for an album you're trying to create?

IDEALS/DREAMS

Some say that everyone is a designer, but not everyone can design. The solutions and ideas that participants share with you offer insight into the hidden problems that you didn't know existed. Problems are hard to describe, and harder to identify. Half-baked solutions are the nondesigner's way of expressing problems they experience. Those pseudosolutions can be inspiration and guidance for your own product.

Example: If you could, how would you incorporate videos and other forms of media in the photo albums you create for your friends and family?

How to Practice Asking Questions

You don't want to say questions out loud for the first time in a research session. This is a common mistake when you're starting out, but is easily avoided. You can practice and iterate your questions by performing a few dry runs with people around the office, and even just speaking into a recorder.

COWORKERS AND DRY RUNS

It's always a good idea to validate your interview guide internally. From the product owner to the engineering team, these are the folks who are putting their time and energy into building a product, and their feedback helps refine and shift your lines of questioning. It's important to reach out to coworkers who may not be directly involved with your product by conducting a full dry run of an interview. Dry runs give you the opportunity to become comfortable asking questions, and to collect constructive feedback that won't negatively impact the data you gather during a session.

Exercise: Brainstorming Questions

Before we move on, we want to share an exercise we use when creating our own questions. This is a quick activity that will allow you to get a ton of questions out of your head and spend more time on the flow of the interview and areas you want to explore.

1. **Grab some sticky notes!**

   Sit down somewhere quiet with a wall that supports sticky notes (whiteboards or any other flat, nonglossy surface) and just start writing down things you'd like to ask about. These could be general topics or specific questions; the important part is you want to get as much out of your head as possible without regard to research goals, project needs, product strategy, or personal curiosity. Limit this activity to 5–10 minutes, or until you've stared at a blank sticky note and no new questions come to mind. (See Figure 2-2.)

FIGURE 2-2
Sample of a sticky-note exercise

2. Challenge each question.

Get all your sticky notes up on the wall so you can see them in one spot. For each note, ask yourself why you need to ask that question, how it ties back to your research goals, and what's influencing you to inquire about it. Also ask what else you could explore that you haven't considered. Grab new sticky notes and write down anything that comes to mind and add it to the wall (Figure 2-3). If you determine that a sticky note doesn't tie back to the research goals or the inquiry, ask yourself how it could be reframed so it does benefit your research efforts. Don't be afraid to take stickies down entirely.

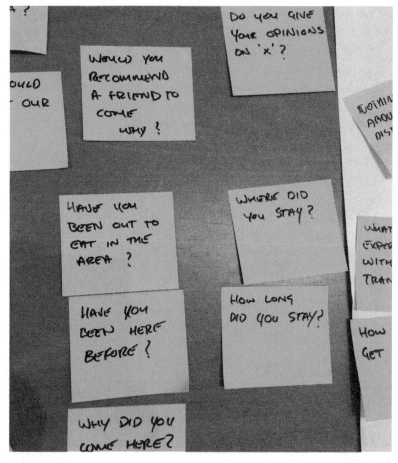

FIGURE 2-3

Additional sticky notes

3. **Take inventory.**

Collect all your follow-up sticky notes and start to store these in some inventory, be it a Word document, spreadsheet, or mindmapping tool. These follow-up stickies are what you're going to use to craft your final list of questions and to guide the order in which you'll ask them. While there is no one right tool, we often use Microsoft Excel, BoardThing, and Trello (Figure 2-4).

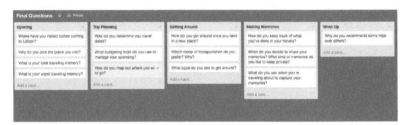

FIGURE 2-4
Sample Trello board as digital sticky notes

4. **Practice!**

We've already talked about how you can practice your research questions, so now's the time to grab that team member or coworker, see how the questions feel, and iterate as needed.

Parting Thoughts

Crafting the questions you need to ask is challenging, and it can dissuade many budding researchers. Don't let the difficulty get you down—it's a natural part of the process of learning a new skill. This is especially true for research. Every researcher from any field has been through the same struggles.

In terms of design, what really matters is that you care enough about your product that you get out of your own way and reach out to people for help. If there's one thing we've learned by doing countless research sessions over the years, it's that people who use or might want to use your product honestly care about its success. They will go on and on about what they love and hate about your product, and this is information you can't get anywhere else.

Now that you know how to structure a question to get the best data, it is important to recognize that there are many different ways questions can be used in research, and many different types of research. Over the course of the next two chapters, we will explore the two main buckets of research: qualitative and quantitative research.

[3]

Quantitative Research Methods

Above all else, show the data.
—EDWARD TUFTE

Now that we've introduced the various types of questions you'll attempt to answer through your research efforts, we'll discuss the two types of research found in product design: quantitative and qualitative research. This chapter and the next introduce the history, variations, and application of these two methods. All successful products rely on the integration of both quantitative and qualitative methods, and there is no silver bullet. Just as different methods require different skills, teams with a variety of skill sets are encouraged.

Quantitative Research by the Numbers

Quantitative research is simply defined as the study of what can be measured and observed. More specifically, quantitative research means the results will be consistent and generally agreed on by all parties involved. Your height and weight are quantifiable measurements, as they can be counted and measured against a standard scale. On the other hand, your personality is a qualitative measurement, as "nice," "kind," and "mean" are all subjective. We will talk more about qualitative research in Chapter 4.

On the Web and in the product space, quantitative measurements may include:

- Bounce rates

- Time on task

- Conversion rates

- Order size (number of items or their value)

- Number of visitors to a site (physical or digital)

- Average size of group

WHERE DO I FIND QUANTITATIVE RESEARCH?

We have all encountered quantitative data, even if it was only in grade school. The most common aspects of quantitative research are mean (the average value), median (the middle value), mode (the most common value), and range (the difference between the highest and lowest values). While helpful for high-level understanding of averages and trends, these numbers only scratch the surface of what quantitative research can provide.

Quantitative research informs designers where customers are accessing their information as well as what devices they are using. In a world where "mobile first" is touted as scripture, quantitative analytics support that claim with actual numbers. In April 2015, Pew Research estimated that 64% of American adults own a smartphone of some kind, and that 10% of Americans use a smartphone as their primary Internet device (Figure 3-1).[1] This is an example of how quantitative research provides primary use cases for modern products with digital components.

FIGURE 3-1

Pew Research chart of mobile usage

1 Aaron Smith, "U.S. Smartphone Use in 2015," Pew Research Center, April 1, 2015 (*http://www.pewinternet.org/2015/04/01/us-smartphone-use-in-2015*).

WHAT QUANTITATIVE RESEARCH IS NOT

While very informative, quantitative research doesn't tell us how to fix things, doesn't tell us why things happen, and doesn't share information that isn't asked for. That being said, quantitative research can act as a benchmark for future studies and for qualitative research.

First, quantitative research doesn't tell us how to fix issues, as it is only a historical representation. Numbers do not consider context of use. For instance, if a thermostat is intended for use in private homes and is installed instead in an industrial setting, issues may occur that would not be properly diagnosed, as the context of use is incorrect and not visible through an analytical readout.

Similarly, quantitative research doesn't tell us why things happen. Did a customer click on a certain link because they didn't visually see the intended goal? Or did they perceive the link as the correct destination?

Lastly, quantitative research shares only information we ask for. Site analytics are good only when they're actively measured. Call center statistics and usage metrics are valuable only if you have them and are able to measure change over time.

Quantitative research is a valuable tool. As we continue to explore the facets of research, keep in mind this is one side of the coin.

Three Focuses of Research

There are three main focuses of research that inform our work as product designers. Though they're commonly called *planning, discovery and exploration,* and *testing and validation,* we describe them here as *insight-driven, evaluative,* and *generative.* While these are distinct and specific areas, they have overlapping characteristics and often span project phases (Figure 3-2). They also go beyond simple product design and ideation, impacting maintenance and support goals for ongoing projects. Remember, design and iterations aren't finished just because a product shipped. And with many of our products going digital, pushing updates is easier than ever. We should always be looking to measure and improve the products we deliver.

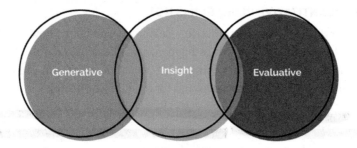

FIGURE 3-2

The three main focuses of research—insight-driven, evaluative, and generative—are distinct yet have many overlapping characteristics

INSIGHT-DRIVEN

Insight-driven research seeks to understand what the problem space is, why the problem exists, and where opportunities lie. Often conducted in early stages of projects, insight-driven research may be as simple as looking at the rate at which your users are succeeding when they attempt to accomplish certain goals. For quantitative research, insight-driven research manifests as benchmarks, often referred to as *key performance indicators* (KPIs). Product teams use KPIs to properly set goals and to measure a product's overall success. KPIs may be conversion rates, new customer or sales numbers, or time spent engaging with a product.

EVALUATIVE

Evaluative research, on the other hand, looks to measure how a design or solution stands up to the KPIs and benchmarks laid out. A user flow is a common artifact that identifies touchpoints and challenges throughout a process. Evaluative research helps answer how this flow is effective both before and after proposed changes. While this kind of research may be done with both quantitative and qualitative measures, quantitative measurements can pinpoint opportunities to improve on a larger scale than qualitative research. For instance, quantitative studies of a healthcare user flow can show how improvements to a system have decreased the time nurses spend entering data and increased the time they spend engaging directly with patients.

GENERATIVE

Lastly, generative research methods offer opportunities to create and explore new designs through research. Often called *data-driven design*, generative research methods balance subjective design recommendations and trends with quantifiable, measurable gains and opportunities. This approach may consider Fitts's law, as discussed in Chapter 1, or may use A/B testing, which we'll discuss in the next section.

Types of Research Methods

There are many types of quantitative research available. The next few sections will highlight a small number of methods and how they support insight-driven, evaluative, and generative project goals. This list is by no means comprehensive, and we encourage you to explore and adapt these methods for your own use.

SYSTEM ANALYTICS

System analytics are probably the most common form of quantitative data. Often referred to as *site analytics* for web-based experiences, analytics provide passive access to a wide array of data points. Analytics are a great example of insight-driven research because of their low cost of entry and, assuming correct tagging on the backend, depth of information. Some of the most common pieces of data include user flows, demographics, and geography.

User flows may be used to understand how customers access and navigate a tool. If your product is a website, are users accessing the product from the home page or through natural search (a search engine)? Are they interacting with your navigation or are they immediately using the search feature (which may be an indicator of poor labeling and tagging, called *taxonomy* among UX practitioners)? You can learn how customers perceive your product and taxonomy through search logs, which highlight their search terms and mental model.

Demographics include age, gender, and other biographical data. This information is particularly helpful for products that target specific user groups—for instance, young investors or users with specific medical conditions.

Geography is particularly helpful in understanding where your customers are coming from. If you want to build a global product and can identify a country or region as a focus for launching your tool, you can build on the successes of an already established market.

There are a number of tools available for gathering and displaying system analytics. Google Analytics is a common one that offers a wide array of customization with an easy-to-read dashboard (Figure 3-3).

FIGURE 3-3

The Google Analytics dashboard provides insights into site traffic and usage

SURVEYS

Unlike analytics, surveys straddle both evaluative and insight-driven methodologies by providing data around not only how a system is used but also how it might meet or fail to meet expectations.

Surveys vary in shape and size. You've likely encountered surveys in the form of pop ups as you browse the Internet, or when a call center asks if you have a few moments to provide feedback after you speak with a representative.

Unlike analytics, surveys take a proactive approach to gathering data. Where analytics passively captures information based on customer usage, surveys allow you to actively collect data through more open formats. Common goals of surveys are to learn about intent and quality of service, or whether expectations were met.

Again, many tools exist to create, capture, and analyze surveys. While we're not endorsing any individual tools, in our own work we've used SurveyMonkey (Figure 3-4), Google Forms, Survs, and ForeSee, among others. Each of these tools offers a unique approach to surveys and varying degrees of customization and data manipulation. We highly recommend exploring each tool individually based on your own needs.

FIGURE 3-4
SurveyMonkey results displayed through visual representations

TREE JACKING

Tree jacking is an example of a generative research method, though it can also be used as an evaluative measure. It is a method of evaluating a system's navigation and terminology. A designer will enter a proposed taxonomy into the system and prompt customers to navigate the information. By clicking through the site map, the designer gathers data on users' expectations and understanding of terms by tracking their path through the tree structure. In this way, designers can quickly generate a new information hierarchy and navigation structure through iterative evaluation of proposed solutions.

Using tools like Optimal Workshop's Treejack (Figure 3-5) is by no means an exact science. With all quantitative methods, the questions asked are just as important as the tool and method being used. Let's consider the task of a housewares-focused ecommerce site. A common navigation structure includes sections called Home, Kitchen, Living & Dining, and Bedroom. If a tree-jacking study asked, "Where would you go for a new kitchen appliance?" the answer is simple. A better question would be "Where would you go for new glassware?"

FIGURE 3-5
Optimal Workshop's Treejack tool

EYE TRACKING

Eye tracking is the process of using cameras to follow a participant's eyes as they scan a page. Limited to screen-based products, eye tracking is particularly effective with ecommerce systems and tools.

One major hurdle with eye tracking is the cost of software and the requirement that participants be brought into a lab that can support the technology. While eye tracking was originally limited to desktop interfaces, new systems are being developed to support it on mobile devices.

Tobii is a leader in building eye-tracking software, the results of which are shown in Figure 3-6.

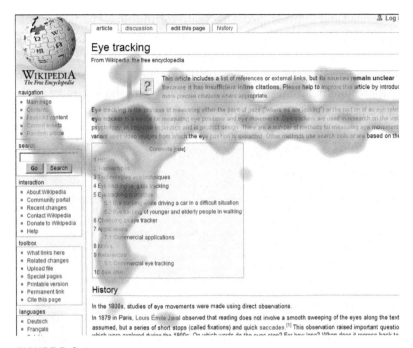

FIGURE 3-6
Sample eye-tracking heat map

A/B TESTING

In A/B testing, a version of site analytics, two different versions of a page are presented to customers. Then, by analyzing the data, researchers can identify a leading option.

A/B testing may be conducted for anything from the color of a button to the headline or body copy of a home page. It is important to focus an A/B test on a specific question and to have established KPIs to measure success with these micro-interactions.

Similar to system analytics, A/B testing is limited in that it provides a retroactive look at behavior but does not provide the subjective "why" or intent of different actions.

CARD SORTING

Card sorting is very similar to tree jacking as a generative research method. Through card sorting, participants arrange topics and items in logical chunks based on their own understanding of the data (Figure 3-7). Variations in card sorting include open and closed, as well as moderated and unmoderated. Open card sorting allows participants to organize cards any way they see fit, while closed card sorting provides predetermined groups or master labels. Card sorting is a fascinating research tool because, depending on the exact implementation, it may be more quantitative (with tools like Optimal Workshop) or more qualitative (with smaller participant groups).

FIGURE 3-7
Sample card sorting exercise

ADDITIONAL METHODS

In Table 3-1 we have organized the quantitative methods just listed, as well as a number of others, highlighting their tendency toward insight-driven, evaluative, or generative approaches to product design. Understanding where these methods fit within a project phase will assist you in selecting the most effective approach throughout your product design.

TABLE 3-1. Quantitative research methods

METHOD NAME	DESCRIPTION	INSIGHT-DRIVEN	EVALUATIVE	GENERATIVE
A/B testing	A method of implementing two solutions and, by displaying them to randomly selected customer groups, determining a preferred solution.		X	
Analytics	Any measure of statistical data or usage of a system. This may include click rates, bounce rates, time on task, and more.		X	X
Card sorting	A method of seeking understanding for a customer's mental model of a system's architecture. May be open (where customers can create their own labels and groups) or closed (where labels and groups are provided).	X	X	X
Customer feedback	Any format of requesting and gathering large-scale customer input.	X	X	
Email surveys	One method for gathering customer feedback.	X	X	
Eye tracking	A lab-based method where cameras track a customer's eye movement across a digital product.		X	
Intercept testing	A method of randomly requesting customer feedback as they engage with a product.	X	X	
Moderated product testing	A method of validating a product with a researcher actively engaging customers.	X	X	X
Surveys	Any format where customers are presented with open or closed questions on their experience with a product.	X	X	
Taxonomy review (tree jacking)	An analytical method to address system architecture and taxonomy.	X	X	
Unmoderated product testing	A method of validating a product with a researcher setting up questions for a customer to respond to at a later time.			

Quantitative Methods: When and Where

Every tool has its place, and quantitative research methods are no different. Quantitative methods are best used when a large number of participants or customers may be accessed for the most statistically significant outcomes. This isn't to say that quantitative methods don't work in smaller studies. Eye tracking and card sorting, for instance, need only a handful of participants to show utility. Still, one of the major distinctions quantitative research has over qualitative research is the larger scale. Additionally, quantitative methods are best employed when the question at hand has a tangible, measurable outcome. A good question for quantitative research might be "How many users abandon the checkout process when signing up for a product's service?" Seeking to understand preference or desirability of a product is less effective for quantitative research than efficacy of a proposed solution.

Quantitative Methods: When to Avoid

Quantitative methods, while valuable, do have some key shortcomings. Despite the variety of quantitative methods, they don't always fit the job.

When you are looking to understand a user's motivations or comprehension of a task, qualitative methods, covered in Chapter 4, offer more tangible results. Similarly, if you have access only to a small number of users, analytics may not be statistically significant. If you're developing a product for an entirely new market, analytics may not exist at all. Without this benchmark, quantitative methods may not be as effective as simply hitting the streets and talking with people face to face.

Voice from the Streets

Matthew Wakeman

In a few words, describe your job.

I've invested my two-decade career in pursuit of customer and business insight—applying marketing research, digital strategy, and digital, customer, and predictive analytics.

How do you use quantitative research?

I'm a digital quant—I analyze digital behavioral and customer data to inform business and experience strategies. Most people think that I spend half my day using Microsoft Excel, a quarter of my day tagging a website, and the remaining bit running advanced statistical models with the latest package for Python or Julia.

It might be nice if it were that way, but that doesn't happen often.

I've had the good fortune to work across several agencies, with clients ranging from two-person startups to Fortune 50 multinationals, and certainly the types of data I've worked with have been different in each scenario. However, heavy-duty modeling or crunching is usually not the largest or the most important part of the job. By far what matters most is defining the key business questions to be answered, and the audiences from which you need the answers. To borrow from people much smarter than me, "If I had only one hour to solve a problem, I would spend up to two-thirds of that hour in attempting to define what the problem is."

Once I have a well-defined question, it's simple to identify which information resources will best answer it, and then collect, merge, and analyze them to answer the question.

It's a little ironic that the first question a user experience designer will ask when we work together is either "What are the top 10 pages on this site?" or "What's the average time on site?" Unfortunately, neither of those questions will help design a better experience.

In my experience, the best questions I've heard are ones like:

- Where in the experience should we focus our design efforts? (This implies identifying what's broken, and prioritizing that list based on critical path and opportunity for improvement.)
- Which audience segments will move the needle for the business?

In terms of basic questions, designers are the best-equipped people to answer "how" to redesign an experience. When it comes to "what," "where," and "when" is an experience being used, those questions should be answered by quants. "Who" and "why"—those are actually questions that need the strengths of both disciplines to be answered.

Exercise: Getting to Know Quantitative Research

In order to best understand quantitative methods, follow this exercise. It shouldn't take more than 15–20 minutes and will allow you to immediately apply some of the ideas discussed in this chapter.

1. **Think of a project.**

   Think of a project you are currently working on. If you are between projects, think back to the exercise in Chapter 2.

2. **Write down what questions you want to answer with your project.**

   On individual sticky notes, write down five questions related to your project that can be answered with hard numbers. This may be "Who uses our system?", "How long do people use the system?", or anything else that comes to mind.

3. **Write down why you want to ask those questions.**

   On separate sticky notes, write why you want to ask each of these questions. Pair each "why" with the appropriate question.

4. **Identify who can help you.**

   Identify who on your team might be able to access this information. Is it a programmer, a data analyst, or even the client? Write down the role and name next to each question.

5. **Make a game plan.**

   Take these questions to work and start a conversation with each of the individuals. Look to understand what it might take to gain the desired information. You might be surprised as to how many of these questions are easily answered or already available. As we shared in Chapter 2, knowing what to ask is as important as asking the right question.

Parting Thoughts

So far we have addressed quantitative research methods and the implications these methods have on product design. Still, this is only a portion of the tools at our disposal. In the next chapter, we will evaluate qualitative research methods and how they can be integrated with the quantitative methods we've discussed here.

Many designers tend to avoid quantitative research, as the idea of statistical analysis can seem daunting. To the readers whose palms sweat at the thought of large data sets, fear not. Many tools offer low-level analysis for free, and many organizations have an Excel guru, even if that guru doesn't want it known. Learning about these tools and identifying these allies is a key piece of your design toolkit.

[4]

Qualitative Research Methods

Objectivity requires taking subjectivity into account.
—LORRAINE CODE

> Quantitative research is the foundation of research. The stories from Chapter 1 illustrate how numbers impact efficiency and worker flow creates an opportunity to innovate product design. As efficiencies in technology reach a predictable flow, designers seek to do more than streamline tasks. They ask what drives people to do the work they do and what makes it enjoyable. Enter qualitative research.

Qualitative Research: Can You Feel It?

Qualitative research is the study of anything that is subjective, notably the personal stories and challenges of our customers. Where quantitative research focuses on what can be measured, such as the time to complete a task, qualitative research looks at why customers are completing the task in the first place. Qualitative research seeks to understand customers' motivations and desires by focusing on comprehension and accessibility that might not be numerically measured, but can nevertheless impact usability and desirability of systems.

Some common measures of qualitative research include:

- Pleasures or challenges of a task

- Preferences for different tools

- Comprehension of content

- Comfort with system or task

- Workarounds, hacks, and "MacGyvered" solutions

This list differs dramatically from the one in Chapter 3. These factors cannot be statistically measured. At the same time, qualitative research provides insights and can use smaller data sets.

WHERE DO I FIND QUALITATIVE RESEARCH?

Qualitative research has roots in ethnography, anthropology, and psychology. The study of how humans behave is, at its core, qualitative research. Compared to the large pools of users researchers rely on to collect quantitative data, qualitative research often relies on smaller participant groups. Projects may have as few as 5–10 participants or, for projects with a broad scope and range of user profiles, upward of 20–40 people.

Qualitative research provides insight into individuals' motivations as well as how they feel toward a product or service. This research provides contextual clues otherwise obscured by data or technology. Take the example of the good old VCR (Figure 4-1). As many readers might recall, VCRs came with a clock display that often flashed 12:00, especially after a power outage. A product designer might quantitatively measure the time required to set up the clock, and would be very disappointed to learn that the time on task is very high and the task is often left incomplete. While informative, this quantitative data set does not reflect the time spent reading the VCR manual or arguing with family members about how to set up this device. Only qualitative research can provide this degree of context and situational awareness. This information, in conjunction with quantitative data, can inform unique design solutions.

FIGURE 4-1
VCRs were notorious for not being programmed

WHAT QUALITATIVE RESEARCH IS NOT

Qualitative research provides the why and the how of human behavior that quantitative methods do not provide. Unlike quantitative research, these are softer skills or details not captured by a spreadsheet. That isn't to say that qualitative research can't exist without quantitative research. In fact, the best projects often succeed from integrating practices of both sides of the research spectrum.

Three Focuses of Research, Revisited

In the previous chapter we defined quantitative research methods as being insight-driven, evaluative, and generative. While this is true for qualitative research methods as well, we want to provide equal time to both ways of defining research—by phase and by type. This chapter will explore research techniques primarily by phase: initial planning, discovery and exploration, and product testing and validation (Figure 4-2).

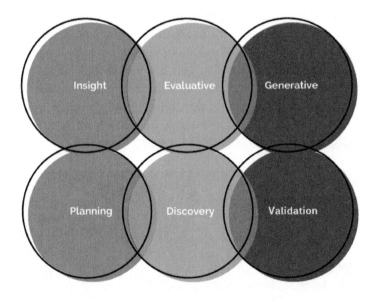

FIGURE 4-2

In addition to insight-driven, evaluative, and generative, another way of looking at research is initial planning, discovery and exploration, and testing and evaluation

INITIAL PLANNING

Initial planning often goes hand in hand with scoping. For those working in-house on internal products or at a startup, this might be the phase where the market needs for a product are evaluated.

Due to the limited scope of this phase, quantitative research is often too expensive or time-consuming to conduct. After all, in a consulting environment scoping exists before a client agrees to a project cost, and it's in everyone's best interest to be sensitive to timelines and to use existing knowledge to form educated guesses. Fortunately, there are low-cost methods for quickly evaluating a project's domain.

Landscape analysis

Landscape analysis, a form of insight-driven research, is one of the most common forms of qualitative research at your disposal. Essential to initial discovery and planning, it requires a minimum amount of time and is crucial to your understanding the market you're designing for.

For a landscape analysis, designers identify existing products or services that reflect a portion of the new product's functions or customer segmentation. For instance, if you are designing the newest transportation service, reviewing how Uber, Lyft, and various car-share services work is essential. It might also be important to evaluate nontraditional services, such as bike-share and carpooling services, and even public transit. By conducting this low-level analysis, the team can identify broad gaps or opportunities for their product (Figure 4-3).

FIGURE 4-3

A landscape analysis is not often formal or fancy; this overvie shows different transportation service options, including Enterprise CarShare, Lyft, Indego Bike Share, and Turo

Landscape analysis is not without its limitations. Often done in iso-lation from business stakeholders and customers, landscape analysis provides a biased view of what the product team identifies as import-ant. It is also limited only to what can be seen from a public view.

Heuristic reviews

Heuristic reviews are the next level of insight-driven research. Performed either at the end of presales or immediately after the project starts, a heuristic review evaluates an existing product or service based on an established set of heuristics, or best practices.

While there are many flavors of heuristics, we recommend choosing from the following list, which offers a wide variety of web and human behaviors to measure against as well as a balance of technical and emo-tive needs (Figure 4-4):

- Jakob Nielsen's 10 Usability Heuristics
  (*https://www.nngroup.com/articles/ten-usability-heuristics*)

- Abby Covert's IA Heuristics
  (*http://abbytheia.com/2012/02/04/ia_heuristics*)

- Weinschenk and Barker Classification of Heuristics
  (*https://en.wikipedia.org/wiki/Heuristic_evaluation#Weinschenk_and_Barker_classification*)

- Gerhardt-Powals' Cognitive Engineering Principles
  (*https://en.wikipedia.org/wiki/Heuristic_evaluation#Gerhardt-Powals.E2.80.99_cognitive_engineering_principles*)

10 Usability Heuristics for User Interface Design

by JAKOB NIELSEN on January 1, 1995

SOURCE: https://www.nngroup.com/articles/ten-usability-heuristics

1. Visibility of system status

   The system should always keep users informed about what is going on, through appropriate feedback within reasonable time.

2. Match between system and the real world

   The system should speak the users' language, with words, phrases and concepts familiar to the user, rather than system-oriented terms. Follow real-world conventions, making information appear in a natural and logical order.

3. User control and freedom

   Users often choose system functions by mistake and will need a clearly marked "emergency exit" to leave the unwanted state without having to go through an extended dialogue. Support undo and redo.

4. Consistency and standards

   Users should not have to wonder whether different words, situations, or actions mean the same thing. Follow platform conventions.

5. Error prevention

   Even better than good error messages is a careful design which prevents a problem from occurring in the first place. Either eliminate error-prone conditions or check for them and present users with a confirmation option before they commit to the action.

6. Recognition rather than recall

   Minimize the user's memory load by making objects, actions, and options visible. The user should not have to remember information from one part of the dialogue to another. Instructions for use of the system should be visible or easily retrievable whenever appropriate.

7. Flexibility and efficiency of use

   Accelerators—unseen by the novice user—may often speed up the interaction for the expert user such that the system can cater to both inexperienced and experienced users. Allow users to tailor frequent actions.

8. Aesthetic and minimalist design

   Dialogues should not contain information which is irrelevant or rarely needed. Every extra unit of information in a dialogue competes with the relevant units of information and diminishes their relative visibility.

9. Help users recognize, diagnose, and recover from errors

   Error messages should be expressed in plain language (no codes), precisely indicate the problem, and constructively suggest a solution.

10. Help and documentation

    Even though it is better if the system can be used without documentation, it may be necessary to provide help and documentation. Any such information should be easy to search, focused on the user's task, list concrete steps to be carried out, and not be too large.

FIGURE 4-4

A sample of common heuristics

Heuristic evaluations seek to identify opportunities and gaps in an existing workflow. While they can be performed with competitor products, it is best to evaluate the product you are looking to improve. While there is no single way to craft a heuristic review, Figure 4-5 illustrates one approach.

Heuristic Evaluation

1. Summary
   Provide a quick summary (1 sentence) of the taks that is performed for this heuristic violation.

2. Page identified
   Provide the URL (or page title) that this heuristic violation is found.

3. Strengths
   Provide any positive factors about the task performed for this heuristic violation.

4. Heuristics violated
   Provide the code of the heuristic (e.g., AC1-Findable) that this task ciolates using the guides found in the Appendix of this document.

5. Details
   Provide any other detail that hasn't been captured above, or, a short recommendation on how to resolve the violation.

6. Screen shot of violation
   Provide a screen shot of the violation.

FIGURE 4-5
A sample template for an individual heuristic violation

DISCOVERY AND EXPLORATION

The discovery and exploration phase is often the focus of product teams. Determining the idea and exploring various avenues and solutions seems to be the most exciting part of our work. Often inline with generative stages of research, discovery offers insights that were previously unobtainable.

Contextual inquiry

Contextual inquiries—also known by names like think-aloud studies and ride-along studies—are easily the most common version of discovery and exploration.

At their core, contextual inquiries are the study of how people perform one or more tasks in context. Redesigning a risk assessment tool for financial traders? Go to the trading floor and sit with the investors.

Designing a new method to handle electronic health records? Visit a physician's office to see how nurses, doctors, and office managers handle data. The goal of contextual inquiries is to be a fly on the wall and observe tasks with as little interference or bias as possible. Where quantitative research methods are conducted passively, contextual inquiries require one-on-one attention to participants and a larger time investment, and must be conducted in person (Figure 4-6).

FIGURE 4-6
Contextual inquiry in the field

While the goal of contextual inquiries is to be as unobtrusive as possible, questions are highly encouraged. Contextual inquiries start with a prompt to participants to "think aloud" about what they are doing. This provides context of actions as well as immediate, observable feedback on their tasks. Researchers often probe, asking questions of the participants to gain deeper understanding (with the caveat that if something is time-sensitive or important, questions can be revisited later).

Contextual inquiries can be conducted with as few as 5 or as many as 50 participants, depending on the project scope. This is a major distinction from quantitative research, where large data pools are the only way to guarantee good data. Contextual inquiries instead rely on trends and the researcher's experience and ability to make judgment calls about what is important. A good rule of thumb: as you start to hear the same information again and again, you have conducted enough research.

PRODUCT TESTING AND VALIDATION

The most important stage of any product design is testing and validation. In common product development cycles, teams move between validation and discovery in a fluid manner, constantly improving concepts. Product testing is most closely tied to evaluative research and also informs generative research.

Moderated product validation

In an ideal world, product validation is conducted in a moderated setting where a researcher is able to meet directly with users of the system. This allows moderators to adjust testing criteria on the fly and ask probing questions as needed.

Moderated product validation often involves inviting participants to a lab, or meeting them in their place of work. They will be instructed to follow a series of specific tasks and, as with contextual inquiries, will be prompted to speak their thought process aloud.

In this way, teams observe in real time how their product behaves with customers and can identify opportunities for improvements. In conjunction with quantitative tests like A/B tests, a holistic view of the system can be achieved.

Unmoderated product validation

It is not always affordable and practical to invite participants to your office. In the case of global products, traveling to different locations may be cost-prohibitive. Tools like User Testing (*https://www. usertesting.com*) provide a great way to quickly and affordably set up remote, unmoderated product testing. While limited to services that can be hosted on the Web, User Testing and similar tools allow moderators to upload a script of tasks. Participants then log in and, using their device's microphone, can think aloud as they walk through predetermined tasks. Screen recordings in conjunction with the audio make a good alternative to moderated testing (Figure 4-7).

FIGURE 4-7
UserTesting.com provides task and instructional information for remote testing

While lower cost and often quicker to deliver feedback, unmoderated validation is limited in that the script is predefined and a moderator cannot adjust a question based on a unique perspective or lessons from previous tests. Unmoderated testing requires additional diligence in crafting questions in order to ensure they are not leading or too prescriptive. A third option for product validation is remote moderated testing, which combines the real-time interaction with customers and the support of digital communication screen-sharing tools such as Skype, Join.Me, or GoToMeeting.

PARTICIPATORY DESIGN

Participatory design takes on many shapes and flavors. This may be as simple as a workshop brainstorming ideas and opportunities, or a more formal sketching exercise. Participants may be asked to sketch actual interfaces or adapt their mental model in visual ways.

Participatory design often takes place with business stakeholders, though it can be used at any phase of research. Collaborative exercises may occur at the end of a contextual inquiry, the closing question of a validation session, or anywhere else the product team has opportunities to collaborate with stakeholders and customers.

ADDITIONAL METHODS

Just as there were more quantitative research methods than could be covered in a single chapter, the breadth of qualitative research spans beyond these pages. Table 4-1 summarizes the methods just covered plus a few additional methods we find particularly helpful.

TABLE 4-1. Qualitative research methods

METHOD NAME	DESCRIPTION	PLANNING	DISCOVERY	VALIDATION
Card sorting	A similar method to quantitative card sorting with smaller pools of available customers.		X	X
Contextual inquiry	An ethnographic approach of following customers in their environment and observing their use of a product or system.		X	X
Diary study	A method, either digital or analog, where customers track their own use and behaviors with a system.		X	X
Heuristic evaluation	An expert review of a system based on established or accepted benchmarks.	X	X	
Landscape analysis	A review of similar or competing products within an industry.	X	X	
Moderated product validation	Similar to quantitative product validation with smaller data sets and a more ethnographic approach.			X
Participatory design	Methods of eliciting design and strategic understanding from customers and stakeholders.	X	X	
Stakeholder workshop	Methods of guiding conversations with business stakeholders on goals and opportunities of a system.	X	X	
Surveys	More informal than quantitative surveys.	X		X
Taxonomy review	Differs from quantitative reviews in that it may be conducted by system experts as an initial evaluation.		X	X
Unmoderated product validation	Similar to quantitative product validation but with smaller data sets and a more ethnographic approach.			X

Voice from the Streets

Sara Wachter-Boettcher,
Wachter-Boettcher Consulting

In a few words, describe your job.

I help organizations make sense of their digital content, articulate and agree on goals, understand users' needs, and ultimately figure out how to deliver content that brings it all together.

How do you use qualitative research?

Which content should you produce? Where should it go? How should it be written and organized? Content strategy is a framework for making those decisions intentionally—for choosing what you'll focus on, and what you'll say no to. But just auditing content and looking at analytics won't answer those questions—or get staff to change how they work. You have to talk to real people, too.

I always start with stakeholder interviews—and not just with senior leaders, but also those who create, edit, and manage content. In my experience, content strategy can't be something I create *for* clients. It's a vision for the future that I establish *with* them—one they'll live out over time. That only happens when people at every level understand the goals, buy into the strategy, and commit to changing how they work.

Stakeholder interviews allow people to open up about their challenges, provide input, and ultimately feel more confident that the resulting plan will actually help them, not just cause more headaches. By holding interviews prior to workshops, I'm also better able to prepare for conflicts, frame the challenge for the session, and start the day with a foundation of trust.

Internal stakeholders are one side of the equation, though. Even in organizations that invest in research, I often see content teams determining their strategy based solely on their company's communication goals—rather than stopping to ask what users want and need.

If your strategy ignores users from the start, any content optimization you do down the line—A/B testing, usability testing, whatever—can only lead to incremental improvements, because you won't know whether your entire proposition misses the mark.

That's why I rely on qualitative insights from real users early on. I like to lead open-ended user interviews or contextual inquiry sessions specific to content work, but we'll also partner with other teams or rely on existing research, if it makes the most sense. Whatever we do, we aim to understand what our users' lives look and feel like: What are their goals and motivations? What's standing in their way or stressing them out? How might our content help them, rather than add to their burden?

This won't tell you whether you should use more bullet points or write shorter headlines. What it *will* do is keep you honest about just how much users have going on that has nothing to do with your product. That helps reframe the conversation to be less about what your organization wants to communicate, and much more about how it fits into real people's lives.

All said, qualitative research allows us to see content problems more clearly and thoroughly, and prevents us from going down a path that's unsustainable for an organization or irrelevant to its users.

Qualitative Methods: When and Where

There is no decision tree for when qualitative methods should be used in place of quantitative methods. In fact, both should be used in parallel. Qualitative methods prove effective when there is a small, identifiable population of customers. For new and novel products where quantitative research might be sparse, qualitative research provides exceptional insights and opportunities. Lastly, qualitative research is a great way to show business stakeholders firsthand what customers are feeling.

Qualitative Methods: When to Avoid

One of the major hurdles qualitative research has is that it is a "soft science." Because it's not based in numbers like its sibling, quantitative research, many business stakeholders don't want to rely on qualitative research alone. To address this, invite stakeholders to observe and participate in qualitative research so they might experience the "aha" moments directly. This turns them into allies and supporters rather than blockers when you're discussing findings with the broader client team. It is important to know your audience and what type of results they are looking for when choosing between quantitative and qualitative research.

Qualitative and Quantitative: A Match Made in Heaven

Quantitative and qualitative research methods are equals, not opposites. You cannot have one without the other. The most successful projects balance the two and inform our product designs.

Just as life imitates art, qualitative and quantitative research inform and imitate each other. There is not a single artifact in product design that you won't improve by integrating both of these techniques.

DATA-DRIVEN PERSONAS

Personas are fictional customers you create to represent various user types. These may include the call center representative, the tech native, or the Luddite. Traditional market segments are typically focused on the numbers (age, gender, geography) of customers. Similarly, classical personas may be generated from a handful of contextual inquiries with no hard data grounding them.

Data-driven personas balance this. By combining the analytical data about who's using a system with the data on users' wants, needs, and motivations you've uncovered through contextual inquiries, you can establish well-rounded data-driven personas.

Figure 4-8 illustrates a common structure for developing data-driven personas.

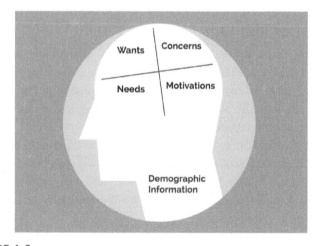

FIGURE 4-8

Draw this diagram on a whiteboard as a basis for your persona, defining user wants, needs, motivations, and demographics

DATA-DRIVEN CUSTOMER JOURNEYS

Customer journeys are often created to illustrate the touchpoints a customer has throughout a process. This may be inclusive of an entire ecosystem, from researching cars online to entering an auto dealership to purchasing the car and making payments. It may also be more specific, such as onboarding for a new piece of technology.

Quantitative customer journeys provide only the steps a customer takes. A qualitative customer journey focuses primarily on emotions. Combining data from both sources allows you to create data-driven customer journeys that account for real task time and latency with awareness of human needs. These can be used as baselines for KPIs and establishing longer-term roadmaps (Figure 4-9).

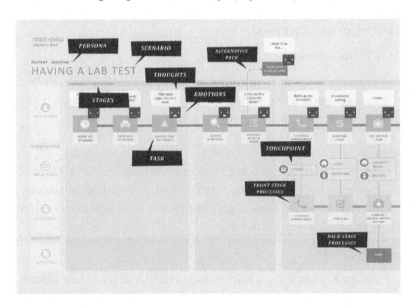

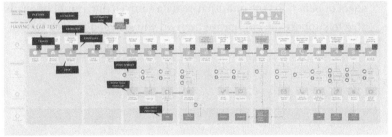

FIGURE 4-9

A representative customer journey map, showing the stages, steps, and touchpoints of a specific test (courtesy of Mad+Pow)

DATA-DRIVEN DESIGN

Data-driven design is the term ascribed to making design decisions with actual data. Rather than basing decisions on customer feedback or design intuition alone, with data-driven design you use system analytics and other data from quantitative research to inform design. There is no single way to integrate quantitative research into design, though we recommend befriending your analytics team and discussing where opportunities to collaborate may exist.

Exercise: Getting the Feel for Qualitative Research

Qualitative research can be a time-consuming process. In order to best understand the opportunities for qualitative research methods in your work, follow this simple exercise to identify the type of research and goals for an existing project.

1. **Choose a method.**

   From the list of methods illustrated in this chapter, select one that you are particularly interested in. Try to identify a method you might not have encountered in a past project.

2. **Write down why you chose this method.**

   Think of a project you are currently working on. On a sheet of paper, list out what you hope to gain from this method. What questions do you have about a project that would be best answered by direct interaction with users?

3. **Bring in data.**

   For many teams, quantitative data is available that can help inform the questions you are asking. If this is true for you, on the same sheet of paper, list the quantitative data sources that might be available to support the qualitative method you selected in step 1.

Parting Thoughts

Qualitative research is often seen as the bread and butter of product design. It doesn't require statistical analysis and employs softer skills that many professionals pride themselves on having. While soft skills and qualitative studies are important, it is equally important to understand when and how to use them. All too often a designer knows only one method and tries to fit that approach into every project. Rather than fit the square peg in the round hole, familiarize yourself with as many methods as possible, and only then focus on a few to become truly proficient in.

With this balance in mind, the next chapter will describe an approach for choosing between quantitative and qualitative research methods. The book will then focus on how research is actually conducted, starting with logistics.

[5]

Choosing Your Methods

But choose wisely, for while the true Grail will bring you life, the false Grail will take it from you.
—GRAIL KNIGHT, *INDIANA JONES AND THE LAST CRUSADE*

Just as important as understanding the breadth of tools at your disposal is knowing when each method may be best utilized and how to adapt methods for your needs.

Quantitative and Qualitative: How to Choose

Having an approach to selecting the right method is critical. Because no two projects are alike, there is no simple, one-size-fits-all way to choose a method, but the following questions will help you define what methods are most appropriate for your given needs.

WHAT ARE YOUR QUESTIONS?

One of the most important factors in determining your research approach is an understanding of what questions you want to ask. This may seem recursive, but just as asking participants good questions is invaluable to product design, challenging yourself to reflect on the same questions in defining a research plan is critical. Are you looking to understand the path customers take using your product? Have you accounted for areas of stakeholder interest that are relevant to the research efforts? Maybe analytics or contextual inquiry can offer insight and clarity. If you are asking why issues arise, diary studies or other surveys may be more conducive to your needs.

STAKEHOLDER NEEDS

Just as important as knowing what questions need to be answered is an understanding of what your stakeholders' goals are. For in-house teams, these goals may align with the designers'. Still, understanding if stakeholders are looking to validate their assumptions, define a new market, or prove their value within an organization helps you define how to address research. Will a quantitative report resonate with your business stakeholders, or will they be more receptive to observing experiences firsthand? How can you best inform stakeholders about the goals and outcomes of your questions?

SAMPLE SIZE

Sample size might be a more binary choice between quantitative and qualitative methods. Based on their roots in statistics, quantitative methods often require large data sets. If you have limited participants available, qualitative methods might be more informative.

If your questions are about the desirability of a feature, you may have access to your entire customer population, and surveys or intercept testing would be most valuable. On the other hand, if you are looking to explore a specific workflow, the customer population may be smaller and qualitative methods would be more appropriate. That said, this guideline is for representative purposes only. Quantitative studies can be performed with small data sets, and similarly, large-scale qualitative studies are common for international products.

SAMPLE LOCATION

Qualitative methods are great for small sample sizes, especially when you can travel to participants in their environment. But with products spanning global markets, travel costs and time may become cost-prohibitive. While many qualitative methods can be used remotely, location is one key factor in determining a research approach.

Unmoderated validation is a great way to span geographical divides, and depending on your timing and goals, you can integrate more quantitative or qualitative approaches into your research plan.

BUDGET

Budget is another limiting factor in choosing methods. Just as location can be cost-prohibitive, specific methods can be as well. If your question is "How are customers navigating through a product?" site analytics provides a low-cost method of retroactively reviewing system usage. Conversely, contextual inquiries may provide more insight and allow for probing questions, though the time investment (approximately 90–120 minutes each) can be difficult to schedule.

TIMELINE

Though the answer to "When do you need to see research results?" is often "yesterday," this is actually a practical question.

Quantitative measures can often be prepared in a set-and-forget mode. For instance, analytics, once enabled, are constantly measured. Card sorting and tree jacking exercises can be enabled and disabled at a whim, and data can be gathered from multiple participants in parallel. Qualitative measures, on the other hand, require more hands-on involvement from researchers and often direct contact with participants, extending the amount of time needed to evaluate the same number of customers.

When choosing a research method, balance the urgency of results with the specialization of various methods. The common saying among product designers is, when considering your constraints of time, budget, and scope (often called the "project triangle"), choose the two that matter most (Figure 5-1).

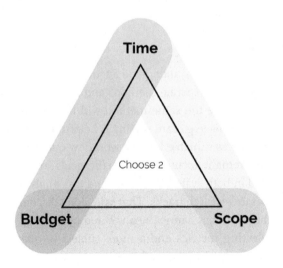

FIGURE 5-1
There are three competing forces in any project; it is common to focus on the most important two and allow the other to be more variable

Mixing and Matching Methods

While a good foundation is important for choosing methods, the best research initiatives borrow from both qualitative and quantitative research methods. We've already discussed many examples, showing their broad use and adaptability within product design. Once you understand how the methods work and have practiced them, feel free to adapt them to make the research process your own.

No method comes ready to use out of the box. Whether because of team dynamics or project challenges, you'll need to adjust methods to meet your specific needs. While we'll discuss some common hurdles, the ultimate goal is to own the research methods and to be willing and comfortable enough to make mistakes while learning along the way.

WHAT WORKS WELL

The best way to combine methods is to understand the root of your question and identify a qualitative and quantitative measure for it. If you're interested in workflow, analytics and contextual inquiries are good options. If you're interested in desirability and feedback, surveys and customer feedback reports are invaluable. In either case, data from one piece of research can be used to inform questions for other research. This process of asking questions, conducting research, and identifying new questions for future use is a key aspect of any successful product team.

WHAT DOESN'T WORK WELL

While merging methods sounds good in theory, it is important not to combine two totally disparate methods and expect valuable results. Similarly, don't assume the same method will be appropriate for two different research goals (e.g., card sorting is helpful for illustrating system structure but less valuable for task workflow questions). Research sessions should remain focused on specific goals and questions. If you're interested in both system structure and task analysis, we recommend two separate research tracks. That said, don't discount new questions simply because they cannot be answered by the current method. If you are collecting metrics and a more subjective question arises, don't be afraid of exploring that path too.

Voice from the Streets

Kevin H. Richardson, PhD

In a few words, describe your job.

I work with clients to scope new projects, mentor my international team (and Sales), and evangelize UX by writing as well as by speaking at meetings and conferences.

How would you summarize the importance and process of research in your work?

As a consulting organization, we specialize in the design of business applications. This means that clients often come to us believing they understand the cause of their problem (poor adoption, high error rates, lengthy training needs, etc.) and have some idea of the solution—even if that solution is simply "a better user experience."

We know, however, that client "problems" are typically indications of deeper issues rather than the root cause. The job of UX is to look beyond the symptoms and determine the underlying nature of the disease.

With this in mind, there are several things we need to know. First, the business requirements and technical constraints. These are straightforward, though we can refine the former via individual stakeholder interviews. After all, clients usually have a pretty good idea of what they want.

Next, and most important, are the user requirements. Ideally, I'll determine the number of users × unique role needed to make a representative sample, and we'll go out into the field, conducting interviews, observations, and contextual inquiries. These methods enable the UX team to determine not only what users say they *want* but also to infer, based on observation and questioning, what they *need*. This is incredibly powerful. People aren't typically able to see beyond their immediate wish list, and the difference between incremental improvement (giving users what they want) and innovation (giving users what they need) lies in skilled requirements elicitation. This means *understanding what users are trying to accomplish* through their interaction with an application, how they work, and how the application in question fits within the larger ecosystem of other applications, tasks, and workflows that make up a typical day.

Without this information, all you have are usability improvements and educated guesses.

Exercise: Choosing an Effective Method

The task of choosing an appropriate research method can be daunting. And while there is certainly more than one way to get to a successful result, this exercise aims to streamline the process of choosing an effective method.

1. **Ask a question.**

   As illustrated, the first step in research is knowing what questions you want to ask. On a blank sheet of paper, write down a question in the center of the page.

2. **Create a mind map.**

   We will now walk through a brief mind-mapping exercise. Start by drawing four lines from the central question, and at the end of each, write down a method or approach to answering that question. You can draw more lines if more ideas are coming to mind, but aim for at least four.

3. **Measure your options.**

   From each response to step 2, draw more lines and write down the risks, opportunities, and needs for each.

4. **Act on it.**

   Review your mind map (Figure 5-2). Share it with a colleague, and discuss a desired method. (While this is a valuable tool for choosing a method, this type of analysis commonly happens only as a mental exercise and is not written down.)

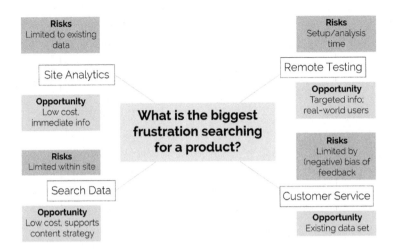

FIGURE 5-2

A sample mind map highlighting risks and opportunities for a fictional ecommerce product

Parting Thoughts

Choosing a research method can be daunting, and you might be tempted to seek a one-size-fits-all approach to product research. Unfortunately, doing this leads to research results that often sound stale, mass-produced, and unconvincing.

The best advice we can offer is to explore as many avenues as possible. Do not be afraid of failure or of asking the wrong questions. Don't worry if the data you collect may not be immediately applicable to your work. Ultimately, there is no such thing as bad research—simply misapplied or poorly structured research. Research is a muscle and, like all muscles, it gets stronger through practice and repetition. To hone these skills, though, you need to know how to actually pull off the research in the first place. We'll talk about that in the next chapter.

[6]

Logistics

As someone who flew two space capsules and twice landed in the ocean, I can attest from personal experience how much logistics work is needed to get you home.

—BUZZ ALDRIN

So far we've talked about how to plan for research, including which methods you'll use and why you should use them. But how do you prepare for the actual days and weeks of research ahead? The logistics of conducting any form of research can appear daunting, but once you have experience, you develop a process for preparation. The content of this chapter is intended to give you a head start by laying out the different things you need to consider, and to provide templates that will help you get going.

Qualitative research requires more preparation than quantitative research. Much of the content presented here pertains to field research and meeting directly with people. Some of the lessons are applied to quantitative methods, and we will call those out so you can be better prepared.

Planning Session Logistics

Before a single research session is conducted, it's important to determine the amount of preparation you'll need for each session, what supplies you'll need, and any travel considerations to be aware of. If conducting research remotely, you'll need to evaluate additional technical constraints. Typical issues could include limitations around phone and web conferencing, prototype bugs, or participants' computer literacy.

SESSION PREP

Every session needs to follow a similar protocol as the other sessions in that study. While information gathered will vary, each session needs to start the same way, have a consistent flow, and generally mitigate risks that could disrupt your session and distract the participant.

Typically, this involves a checklist review before each day of research, before and after each session, and at the end of the day. This checklist includes logistics around setting up sessions, reviewing paperwork, familiarizing yourself with participants, addressing technology hurdles, preparing observers, and gathering supplies.

Session setup

Regardless of whether you're conducting research in a conference room or in a person's house, you'll want to set up your tools and materials before the session begins. This ensures you aren't distracted getting things ready and helps put the participant at ease since you'll convey professionalism and confidence.

Paperwork review

Do you have all the printouts you need for the day? Are they in order? If your paperwork is disorganized, your confidence will get rattled and you can damage the quality of the session. Some forms are required, such as consent or nondisclosure agreements (NDAs), in order for a session to start. Simply put, have all paperwork sorted before meeting with the first participant.

Participant familiarization

Depending on how participants are recruited, which we will detail in Chapter 7, you may have a participant breakdown or cheat sheet. This includes summary information from the recruitment screener. Reviewing this information before participants show up lets you refer to them by name, ask tailored questions to ease them into the session, and gives you clues into areas you want to probe during the actual session.

Tech check

Perform tech checks before and between sessions to ensure potential points of failures don't pop up during your sessions. This is vital when you're conducting research remotely, if you have remote observers, or if you are testing a prototype. Be aware of all existing issues so you can address them during your sessions and help participants navigate past them. If you know where the prototype will cause issues, you are better prepared to address them when they happen during the sessions.

Observer orientation

For many stakeholders, observing UX research in any form is a new experience. Prior to starting sessions, you may need to review key rules observers should follow while sessions are taking place. If observers are in the room with the participant, these rules need to spell out what kind of behavior you expect. This will ensure observer bias is limited. See Chapter 8 for some basic ground rules for observers.

Supplies list

There are common supplies you'll need when conducting qualitative research. Some supplies differ based on the research method you're using, but we've attempted to create a sample list in Table 6-1.

TABLE 6-1. UX research supplies list

SUPPLY	DESCRIPTION
Notebook	You can use this to keep track of additional questions you might want to ask. Observers can also use one to write down their own thoughts and notes, which might be handy later on during the analysis phase.
Sticky notes	An indispensable tool to every designer and researcher when random thoughts need to be collected during research sessions.
Batteries and charging cables	If you are using handheld recorders, your batteries will die at some point.
Voice recorder	Notes sometimes are misleading or don't have all the detail you need, so being able to consult a voice recording is invaluable.
Video recorder	Video is a powerful tool when it comes to reporting out your research results.
Pens	Pens are always handy for signing forms and jotting down notes.
Forms and discussion guide	This comprises all the forms and copies of your discussion guide for yourself, note takers, and observers.
Sharpies	These come in handy when you, the participant, or the note takers want to sketch out an idea.
Memory sticks	It's always a good idea to keep one or more backups of your notes and recordings as the research is being conducted.
Snacks	Provide small snack packs for you and your team to keep your energy reserves up.

SESSION CLEANUP

Sessions require setup and, between participants, cleanup and preparation for the next person. During this time, save any recordings and prepare the recording devices for the next session. Reset prototypes or products you might use and work with your note takers to save notes in the same space as the recordings. The goal is for the next participant to see no evidence of past participants.

Resetting yourself

Take the time between sessions to realign your mind and body. Research is draining, and every participant deserves the same level of attention and energy. Take time to give yourself a mental and physical recharge. This might mean having a coffee, spending five minutes on social media, or reading a page or two of your current book (we are both fans of James S. A. Corey's *Expanse* book series if you happen to be a science fiction fan). This mental break is different for every person. You need to make it part of your process so you avoid burnout and don't miss key details. In addition to the mental break, you might want to have a quick debrief discussion with your team. We cover these conversations in detail in Chapter 12.

TRAVEL CONSIDERATIONS

Not all research is conducted from your office. The best qualitative research is in the field, meeting people where they are. When traveling away from home, map out plans ahead of time and how long it might take to get between sessions. Err on the side of caution and plan for more time than needed, even if that means an extra night in the hotel and catching a morning flight home.

Lunch

With the focus on research and maximizing feedback, it's easy to forget about something as simple as lunch. There have been many times we've skipped lunch because a session went over time or we simply lost track of the day. Learn from our mistakes and give yourself time each day to eat and take care of yourself.

Traffic

Traffic comes in two forms. The first, and standard, form of traffic includes planes, trains, and automobiles. This is easy to research and plan for. The second form of traffic involves micro interactions with other people—in hallways, elevators, parking lots, and security lines. Again, err on the side of safety and always plan for the worst-case scenario. Fortunately, in today's age of immediate Internet access, tools like Google Maps can help you plan trip times, and even set your planned departure time (see Figure 6-1).

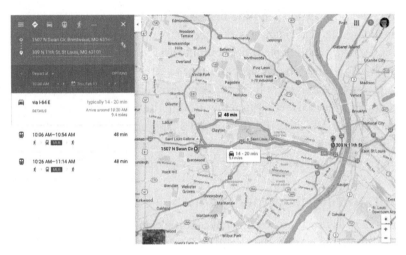

FIGURE 6-1
Google Maps with custom trip time

REMOTE CHALLENGES

With remote research, the risk of something going wrong before or during a session increases. Why? Because technology is a fickle beast and Murphy's law suggests it's best to be extra prepared. Some things to consider having in place include:

- Telephone conference bridge

- Copies of questions ready to email to participants

- Secondary access product or prototype

- Alternative discussion guide or questions

- Printouts and analog versions of anything that isn't entirely dependent on technology

Training participants

One of the first lessons you'll learn after conducting remote research for the first time is that most people don't use online messaging tools on a daily basis. Shocking, right? This is easy to forget; as *designers immersed in technology*, we are used to having these tools at hand.

You should plan to spend the first 5–10 minutes of a remote session ensuring the participant has the necessary connections for an online conferencing tool. Explain how to mute and unmute their audio, how to show and hide their video, and how to either share their screen or request control of yours if you're doing any sort of usability testing. If conducting unmoderated usability testing, be sure introductions and instructions are clear and the content is appropriate for the audience. This helps put the participant at ease and addresses technical issues they might experience so it doesn't distract from the conversation later.

Supporting Documentation

The next few sections will introduce some common artifacts you'll be creating while you plan out your research. The first of these is a welcome kit that can be sent to participants prior to their session. This is a set of documents explaining in detail what they got recruited to be part of, who you are, and how they can validate that the research activity is legitimate.

WELCOME KIT

Welcome kits are great to introduce participants to the research team, and are most appropriate for qualitative in-person methods. Welcome kits are effective if the topic of research is sensitive in nature, as it helps put participants at ease. Common research topics may include financial information, personal health records and history, or topics that might involve their children or loved ones.

Kits should arrive at least three to four days before your scheduled session to give participants plenty of time to digest the information and to prepare for your visit. This may include locating files if you are researching a medical or financial product, or photo albums for a social tool. The content of a welcome kit is illustrated in Figure 6-2.

· Natural Headshots
· Actual members of the reseach team

 · Basic information on the project
· Purpose of the research

 · Include email, phone number, and address

 · Stakeholder contact
· Customer service numbers

FIGURE 6-2
A common foundation for building a welcome kit

What and why

Include basic information on the project, a history of the product, and your reasons for conducting research. Participants now understand how their information is going to be used and why.

Team members

Write up short biographies of the team members conducting the research, along with their contact information. It's also helpful to include photos for in-person sessions so that participants know and recognize you before meeting. If the plan or team changes, it's important to update participants, as they will be expecting to see specific people the day of the session.

Points of contact

Research scammers exist, and sadly it's one way people have their identity stolen. Include a customer service number or point of contact the participant can call to validate that the research is legitimate.

Logistics

Provide a timetable of your arrival and when the session will end. This allows participants to schedule their day around the session, including securing child care or shuffling any other personal appointments.

Voice from the Streets

Ron Strawbridge,
Senior Director of Member Experience,
Express Scripts

When is one time the risks of poor planning were dangerous to your work?

Ninety-six stakeholders, a large conference room in New York, Japanese culture shock, and no solid plan other than to show the client what we do...

Two years ago, I stood across from our engagement leader in this very scenario and heard him say, "You got this, right?" as multitudes of suits piled into a corporate meeting space to share their well-thought-out business insights with me and the project team.

Then I heard the overhead speaker crack. Several more stakeholders were dialing in from overseas, and even more stakeholders were filing into the already packed conference room, all waiting to educate me on the ways of their business. This was not going to go very well.

How was I going to listen to them all? How were we going to attempt a card sort with folks in Asia? How was I going to learn the business strategy from now more than 100 individuals representing 50+ business interests?

It was enough to scare any user experience practitioner—regardless of how well seasoned he or she may be.

We did the best we could in that moment. We assigned note takers and broke the 100+ stakeholders into pods of 25 to work together. Then, the pods reviewed the output from the other pods.

But time was our enemy.

The analysis was overwhelming and took weeks to organize, let alone analyze. We were constantly behind. We brought on more resources, but just getting those resources up to speed was more strain on the team when we were already stretched beyond capacity.

No one wants situations like these, but addressing them up front with a logistical strategy to UX design makes all the difference.

I believe UX design is like solving a math problem. If you approach the problem incorrectly or without mindful thought from the beginning, then your entire solution may be false—or at best ineffective.

"Logistics" are not just for trucking companies or soldiers of fortune. Mindfully planning and designing research means leveraging logistics to help you find the gems you need to take back, refine, and analyze.

The suggestions inside this book will help you do just that.

To be successful, we must practice in ways that force us to relish not just the design of a thing, but also the process of uncovering an understanding of what we are about to design.

Next time I will know to not just think about the activities I am going to conduct, but also be extra mindful about orchestrating the where, when, and how these understanding activities ought to take place.

RESEARCH GOALS

As part of the overall research planning, your team will have defined why they are doing research. For both posterity as well as transparency, it's good to write down your goals for performing research. These can be outlined in a research summary document, in the statement of work, or on a large poster board in a project room. The point is to make your goals visible and documented so everyone is on the same page, both literally and figuratively. This is true regardless of the method, quantitative or qualitative, as having documented goals focuses the team when it comes to analyzing the data collected.

An added benefit of documenting research goals is to include stakeholders. Stakeholders can comment and refine research goals while offering the filters to observe sessions. These filters are handy when you're reporting findings because stakeholders are reminded what the research focused on and, more importantly, what it didn't focus on. While the ways to define goals are endless, we've outlined some common ones.

What will be learned?

Quite simply, state what you want to learn by doing the research. For example: How do people prepare for retirement at different stages of their life?

Why do you need to learn it?

The why of research is sometimes difficult to state as succinctly as the what. Some guiding questions to define the why are: How is the target of the research tied to the product's overall business strategy or the company's culture? What risks will you be taking on by *not* learning about specific topics?

What's your hypothesis?

Here is your chance to include a little bit of the scientific method. Write down assumptions on the outcomes you expect to see. This doesn't need to be long; simply stating, "We expect customers to find the authentication process cumbersome and expect the payment process to be straightforward" is sufficient. Now with this hypothesis documented, aim to prove it wrong. The purpose of research isn't to prove your assumptions right, but to uncover truth in order to solve the real problem.

DISCUSSION GUIDE

In Chapter 2, we went over how you come up with good questions for research and what pitfalls to avoid. The discussion guide is the repository for all questions you want to cover during a research session and presents an ideal order in which to ask them. While discussion guides change from project to project, we've outlined common sections for your convenience.

Opening script

This is a script that you'll read at the beginning of each session to give yourself some form of consistency. The information covered includes:

- Who you are

- Project background

- Reason for the research

- Explanation of participant's value to the goals

- Disclaimer that the participant can end the session at any time

- Expectations for how long the session will last and how participants will be compensated for their time

Screener recap

It's good practice to revisit some of the questions that were presented in the recruitment screener (the specifics of which we'll cover in Chapter 7). It will remind participants why they were recruited and give you hints on areas to ask probing questions. These are also easy questions to answer, so it gets the participants used to you asking them for information.

Research questions

This is the bulk of your discussion guide and the home for the questions defined earlier in your preparations. You'll want to break the questions up based on topic and flag those that are meant as follow-up. It's good practice to assign time blocks to help remember when is a good time to move to the next topic.

CONSENT FORMS

One of the more awkward moments of research sessions involves signing consent forms. These forms are often required before research takes place and can bring legal ramifications if participants don't understand what they are signing. Not every research effort involves all of the following types of consent forms, but it's good to understand them in the event you need to explain them to participants. We encourage participants to read these documents in detail and plan for extra time so they can be as thorough as they wish.

Nondisclosure agreements

No product team wants news about their product to be leaked to the press or their competitors. If you are working on a product, or an enhancement to an existing product, you'll want to have an official nondisclosure agreement (NDA) for the participant to sign (see Figure 6-3). This document legally prevents participants from talking about what they see or do during the session.

NON-DISCLOSURE AGREEMENT

THIS AGREEMENT (the "**Agreement**") is entered into on this ____day of _____ by and between _____, located at _____ (the" **Disclosing Party**"), and _____ with and address at _____ (the "**Recipient**" or the "**Receiving Party**").

The Recipient hereto desires to participate in discussions regarding _____ (the "**Transaction**"). During these discussions, Disclosing Party may share certain proprietary information with the Recipient. Therefore, in consideration of the mutual promises and covenants contained in this Agreement, and other good and valuable consideration, the receipt and sufficiency of which is hereby acknowledged, the parties hereto agree as follows:

1. **Definition of Confidential Information.**

(a) For purposes of this Agreement, "**Confidential Information**" means any data or information that is proprietary to the Disclosing Party and not generally known to the public, whether in tangible or intangible form, whenever and however disclosed, including, but not limited to: (i) any marketing strategies, plans, financial information, or projections, operations, sales estimates, business plans and performance results relating to the past, present or future business activities of such party, its affiliates, subsidiaries and affiliated companies; (ii) plans for products or services, and customer or supplier lists; (iii) any scientific or technical information, invention, design, process, procedure, formula, improvement, technology or method; (iv) any concepts, reports, data, know-how, works-in-progress, designs, development tools, specifications, computer software, source code, object code, flow charts, databases, inventions, information and trade secrets; and (v) any other information that should reasonably be recognized as confidential information of the Disclosing Party. Confidential Information need not be novel, unique, patentable, copyrightable or constitute a trade secret in order to be designated Confidential Information. The Receiving Party acknowledges that the Confidential Information is proprietary to the Disclosing Party, has been developed and obtained through great efforts by the Disclosing Party and that Disclosing Party regards all of its Confidential Information as trade secrets

(b) Notwithstanding anything in the foregoing to the contrary, Confidential Information shall not include information which: (i) was known by the Receiving Party prior to receiving the Confidential Information from the Disclosing Party; (b) becomes rightfully known to the Receiving Party from a third-party source not known (after diligent inquiry) by the Receiving Party to be under an obligation to Disclosing Party to maintain confidentiality; (c) is or becomes publicly available through no fault of or failure to act by the Receiving Party in breach of this Agreement; (d) is required to be disclosed in a judicial or administrative proceeding, or is otherwise requested or required to be disclosed by law or regulation, provided that the requirements of paragraph 4 hereof shall apply prior to any disclosure being made; and (e) is or has been independently developed by employees, consultants or agents of the Receiving Party without violation of the terms of this Agreement or reference or access to any Confidential Information.

2. **Disclosure of Confidential Information.**

From time to time, the Disclosing Party may disclose Confidential Information to the Receiving Party. The Receiving Party will: (a) limit disclosure of any Confidential Information to its directors, officers, employees, agents or representatives (collectively "**Representatives**") who have a need to know such Confidential Information in connection with the current or contemplated business relationship between the parties to which this Agreement relates, and only for that purpose; (b) advise its Representatives of the proprietary nature of the Confidential Information and of the obligations set forth

. . .

(g) The receipt of Confidential Information pursuant to this Agreement will not prevent or in any way limit either party from: (i) developing, making or marketing products or services that are or may be competitive with the products or services of the other; or (ii) providing products or services to others who compete with the other.

(h) Paragraph headings used in this Agreement are for reference only and shall not be used or relied upon in the interpretation of this Agreement.

IN WITNESS WHEREOF, the parties hereto have executed this Agreement as of the date first above written.

Disclosing Party   **Receiving Party**

By_____   By_____
Name: Name:
Title: Title:

FIGURE 6-3

Sample NDA

Permission to record

When you wish to record a session, it is best to capture a participant's agreement by asking them to sign a waiver allowing you to do so (Figure 6-4). In some states, law might require this waiver. This document includes a description of how your team will use the recording. It's important to stress that recordings are a backup to written notes and will never be shared outside the immediate product team. Some people don't like to be recorded, and that's OK. If this happens, show the participant all recording devices are put away and then proceed with the session.

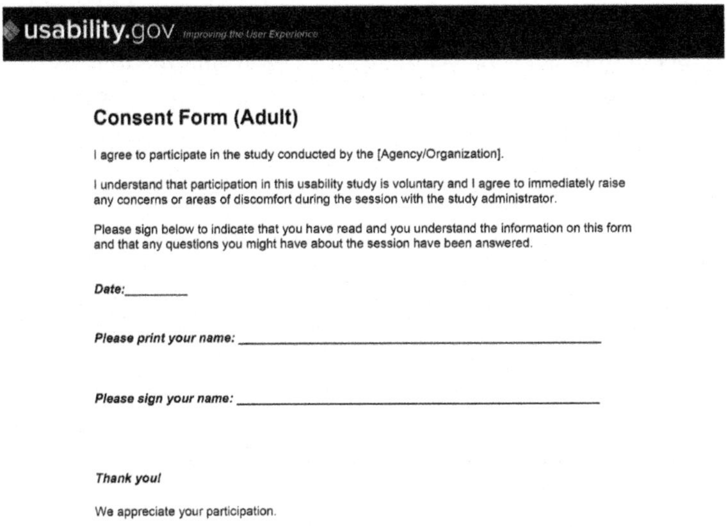

usability.gov *Improving the User Experience*

Consent Form (Adult)

I agree to participate in the study conducted by the [Agency/Organization].

I understand that participation in this usability study is voluntary and I agree to immediately raise any concerns or areas of discomfort during the session with the study administrator.

Please sign below to indicate that you have read and you understand the information on this form and that any questions you might have about the session have been answered.

*Date:*_____

Please print your name: _____

Please sign your name: _____

Thank you!

We appreciate your participation.

FIGURE 6-4
Sample "permission to record" form

Permission to quote

Another form to include asks permission of the participant to use any of their quotes when you report the research findings. Participants should understand that you'll do your best to ensure that any quotes you use will not be identifiable. While not required, this form is a courtesy so people understand how your team may use their words and information.

Honorarium

The majority of qualitative and some quantitative research methods include an honorarium for participating in your research. This reward can incentivize potential participants when you're recruiting and helps reduce "no shows" during sessions. There are a number of ways to handle honorariums, and it's important that the value and type of honorarium is communicated to participants prior to their session. Setting expectations avoids negative feelings, especially when delivery of an honorarium is delayed in the instance of email delivery.

Cash

Cash is by far the easiest form of reward and often the most appreciated. Before your sessions begin, have the cash split in envelopes, one for each participant. This is more secure, as participants won't see a large stack of cash.

Gift cards

Gift cards are often used in place of cash for accounting purposes and are handed out at the end of a session. It is best to provide generic, prepaid cards (e.g., Visa), though if the reward amount is small (typically under $20) there is nothing wrong with providing gift cards to a coffee shop. If vouchers are distributed through email instead of in person, it's important that participants understand when they will receive an email, where it will come from, and how they can use it.

Free product

For product teams that have one or more existing products, a common reward is the product itself. If the product is new, you can advertise something else your team offers in its place. For example, a team creating a new wearable fitness product may offer an earlier version of their product as a thank-you.

Receipts

Regardless of the form, participants should be asked to sign a receipt stating they received their honorarium. This best practice prevents anyone coming back and saying they were not compensated.

Parting Thoughts

Getting logistics right is a challenge for just about every type of research you'll conduct. This topic could be a book all by itself, but the one thing we can promise is that it does get easier in time. The more research activities you plan, the more you learn what will work for your team and what won't. You just have to do what every good designer does naturally: take in feedback on the process and iterate for next time.

As a last piece of advice regarding logistics, remember to be flexible with your plan. The universe likes to mess with everyone, so don't let little issues get you down, as you're probably the only one that will notice. Roll with the punches as they come and keep working your plan to get the information your team needs to make your product better for its users. Speaking of which, our next chapter will discuss recruiting participants who use, or could use, your product and provide valuable insights.

[7]

Recruiting

My name is Harvey Milk, and I'm here to recruit you.
—HARVEY MILK

It's hard to conduct user research if you don't have anyone to research. Recruitment lets you find people that have the information you seek to learn. Recruitment is risky since the effort hinges on getting the right people in the room. There are a number of factors at play, and various methods a team can use to find the right kind of participants. Before worrying about the risks and before scheduling participants, you first must document whom you want to recruit.

Participant Identification

One of the first activities your team will do when planning recruitment is identify participants to recruit. It's helpful that most projects have existing information on customers, giving your team a jump-start on identifying whom you want to recruit and, more importantly, why you want certain types of people to be involved in the research. Common sets of data to identify participants include:

- Past qualitative research

- Current analytic reports

- Customer segments

- User profiles

PAST QUALITATIVE RESEARCH

If there is preexisting research on your product, refer to the existing materials. Your approach should be one of validation. Ask what is missing from the participant criteria. If a different team conducted the research, ask them how the participants mapped to their needs and what they might do differently in a new round of recruiting.

CURRENT ANALYTIC REPORTS

There is a wealth of knowledge about users hidden in the analytics mentioned in Chapter 3. Depending on the details, you can quickly learn where users are geographically, or what personal demographics are important. Analytics can expose gaps in your target demographics and identify opportunities to reach out to underrepresented user groups.

CUSTOMER SEGMENTS

One source of information that's easily overlooked is customer segments organized by marketing teams. Good customer segments are based on purchased data sets or those collected internally and should not be discounted.

USER PROFILES

If your team doesn't have personas from quantitative and qualitative data, you will need to write baseline user profiles to guide recruitment (see Figure 7-1). A user profile is handy for a variety of situations, not just for recruitment. By taking time to document user profiles, you can generate future personas with more ease. User profiles can be shown to stakeholders for review, ensuring recruits align with a stakeholder's presumptions. If there is disagreement, you can resolve this prior to recruiting.

This can be an educational moment for stakeholders who may not be familiar with product research. Because our focus is on behaviors less than demographics, user profiles can complement and validate existing marketing research, as you will be approaching the same subject matter, just from a different point of view.

Sam Smith

Professional Photographer

Age | 32
Type | Primary
Role | Customer

" I got into photography to capture the world around me and to find the stories that only I can see. **"**

Goals

· Make time to explore and take pictures
· Get feedback on recent shoots to improve skills
· Discover mentors to lean new techniques
· Travel to new places to see new sights
· Become more focused on personal style

Behaviors

· Learn ins and outs of equipment
· Always be aware of light levels
· Respects their subject always
· Understands personal photographic goals
· Always carries a camera

FIGURE 7-1

A sample user profile captures demographic information, goals, and behavioral information about a user type

Breaking down profiles

After collecting information about the type of people you'd like to include, you need to break that information down by referring to your research goals and the goals of the product as a whole. You may end up with an overwhelming number of profiles and you can't recruit for all of them. Before creating your *recruitment screener*, a short survey to find people, your team will need to prioritize profiles so everyone knows the importance of different audiences.

There are a number of ways to measure priority. One method is to look for those users the team feels are most likely to interact with the product on a regular basis. Another way to evaluate priority is to focus on reaching users that do not yet use the product. Refer back to the underlying goals to guide the prioritization, and you should have the profiles you want to recruit against.

Identifying key behaviors

User profiles aren't all about demographics and potential lifestyle decisions. One key component of a good user profile is listing existing or potential behaviors (see Figure 7-2). To get this list of behaviors, refer to the goals your product seeks to help users accomplish, as mentioned in Chapter 2. Now, think through the actions and behaviors someone would go through to accomplish those goals given today's world and the different forms of technology they use.

Some common examples include:

- Does the person prefer to shop using a mobile app or desktop website?

- Does the person compare product reviews when making a new purchase? Do they seek information online or in store?

- Where is the person using the product? At home, their office, or in transit?

You'll screen against these actions and behaviors when recruiting users. Your team can prioritize this list of behaviors based on frequency, impact, risk, and any other factors that might influence someone's resulting experience from using a product to accomplish their goals.

Primary Behaviors

Schedules a photoshoot once a month

Uses mid-range to high-end digital cameras

Follows an established workflow with photos

Uses online storefronts to sell photography

Secondary Behaviors

Uses social networks to create fan base

Creates photo albums for friends and family

Participates in the photography community to mentor others and to find mentors

FIGURE 7-2

While key behaviors can simply be represented on a whiteboard, this illustration provides further context for communicating with stakeholders

Recruitment Screener

Recruitment screeners (see Figure 7-3) are internal documents defining what user profiles you plan to research. They provide a consistent basis for your team or external vendors to recruit against and ensure more cohesive data sets.

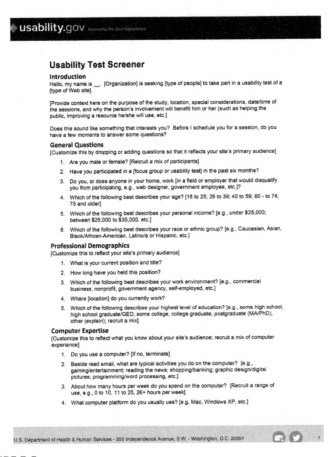

FIGURE 7-3

Sample usability screener

While it can be tempting to skip screening and conduct research with a friend, family member, or someone off the street, such an approach will expose you to risks and gaps in your findings. For instance, if you're researching an online Medicare application form and evaluating college students, the quality of data isn't going to help the team. College students don't have the context, life experience, or understanding of the subject matter to help.

Screening is universal across all research methods. The better you screen, the better your data will be. And quantitative research supports screening too. Passive triggers—such as purchasing a product, using an ISP's location, or visiting a minimum number of pages on a site—may be set off before a survey is presented.

WHAT SCREENERS LOOK LIKE

Recruitment screeners are often surveys consisting of multiple-choice questions. While the number of questions varies, a screener should take no longer than 10–15 minutes to complete. With screeners, shorter is always better, regardless of method (in person, over the phone, or online).

Multiple-choice questions allow a binary decision to be made: certain responses disqualify a participant, while others confirm their desirability. Standard usability screeners (Figure 7-4) are very similar to the screener presented in a summons for jury duty (Figure 7-5).

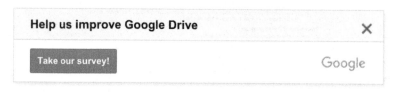

FIGURE 7-4
Sample short screener using Google Forms

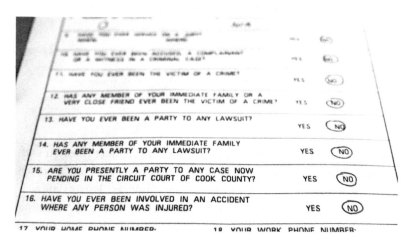

FIGURE 7-5
Sample real-world screener in the form of a juror summons

BASIC DEMOGRAPHICS

Key demographics—such as age, lifestyle, education, and income levels—play an important role in recruiting, since some products may appeal only to a certain user group. Demographics allow you to quickly narrow down the pool of potential participants to those that are more likely to exhibit the behaviors you can learn from.

BEHAVIORAL DEMOGRAPHICS

While basic demographics establish a baseline for recruitment, behavioral demographics establish the filter to ensure participants have the information and experience needed to inform the product's design. One example of a behavioral demographic is someone's online shopping habits. Are they more likely to look in store and buy online? When do they decide to buy online versus in a store?

Or to use a more complicated example: Does this person attempt to resolve issues online first when they have a question? At what point do they feel the need to contact a help line for assistance from a human?

QUOTAS

Time waits for nobody. And with deadlines determining how much time can be spent on research, teams define quotas of how many participants to research from various user profiles (see Figure 7-6). Quotas are also helpful to have after you've defined whom you want to speak to. The potential audience of brain surgeons is significantly smaller than people looking for a new car, and understanding the available participant pool is helpful to avoid overreaching.

Assuming participant availability is not an issue, qualitative research generally targets three to five users per user group. These numbers shift based on how important it is to hear from a specific user profile and how difficult it might be to find people that align with one of your profiles. Remote, unmoderated tests and quantitative research methods may see as many as hundreds or even thousands of participants.

These quotas can be sprinkled throughout a screener survey. As the recruiter works through the screener, some questions with more than two potential responses can have numbers associated with those responses. These numbers ensure you meet with people that matter and your participant pool isn't skewed.

These numbers will tell the recruiter that you want to recruit, say, five people that are heavy online shoppers, and three people that are moderate online shoppers.

Hello, I'm _____ from _____, a marketing research firm. We're looking for individuals to participate in a paid market research study. Your individual answers will not be divulged to anyone, nor will you be asked to purchase anything. Your opinions are very important and we would appreciate your cooperation.

1. CONFIRM GENDER BELOW **(DO NOT ASK, confirm by voice)**
    [ ] Male   CONTINUE (Max of 5)
    [ ] Female   CONTINUE (Max of 5)

2. We are interested in talking to people with a variety of backgrounds. Do you or does any member of your immediate family work for any of the following types of companies?
    (READ LIST, IF YES TO ANY LISTED BELOW, TERMINATE)

    [ ] Marketing Research
    [ ] Advertising
    [ ] Public relations firm
    [ ] Media (i.e., TV, radio, entertainment industry, newspaper)
    [ ] Manufacturer or Retailer of Consumer Electronics
    [ ] Distributor/Manufacturer/Retailer of movies/music/games
    [ ] Creative Agency

3. Have you participated in any consumer research study in the past 3 months?
    Yes   ( ) **TERMINATE**
    No   [ ] **CONTINUE**

4. Are you currently receiving your medications using home delivery?
    Yes   [ ] **CONTINUE**
    No   ( ) **TERMINATE**

5. How do you manage your home delivery medications?
    [ ] Over the phone   **ASK QUESTION 6 (MAX 5)**
    [ ] Through the mail   **ASK QUESTION 6 (MAX 5)**
    [ ] Online   **SKIP QUESTION 6 (MAX 5)**

6. If you could manage your home delivery medications using a website would you?
    Yes   [ ] **CONTINUE**
    No   ( ) **TERMINATE**

7. Do you currently get your prescription medication through Acme? **RECRUIT A MIX, MOSTLY YES**
    Yes   [ ]
    No   ( )

8. *(If current Acme Customer)* How long have you been getting your prescription medication through Acme?
    RECRUIT MOSTLY FROM A-C, D-F ONLY USED AS BACKUP
    [ ]   a. Not an Acme Customer
    [ ]   b. Switching to Acme This Year (2011)
    [ ]   c. 1 – 2 Years
    [ ]   d. 2 – 3 Years
    [ ]   e. 3 – 4 Years
    [ ]   f. 5+ Years

FIGURE 7-6

Sample document illustrating the quotas for different user types

Recruitment Methods

The best method of recruitment identifies quality participants. There are a number of common techniques to generate a participant pool. Some methods take significant time and effort, while others can be implemented quickly.

INTERNAL VERSUS PUBLIC RECRUITING

It's important to address the differences between recruiting participants for an internal product compared to a product for the general public. Internal recruiting seems easier than public recruiting, since you have a relatively captive audience: colleagues within the organization.

One factor impacting internal recruitment is the support of management. If you face the common challenge of management blocking access to employees, rather than get frustrated, involve managers at all levels early in planning. Having a voice in the process encourages managers to contribute both their time and their direct reports' time. This is paramount when you are recruiting time-sensitive or ultra-specialized participants in organizations where even an hour-long session may seem detrimental to a manager.

When recruiting from the general public you lose direct access to participants, but there are a variety of recruiting methods available to streamline the task, which we outline next.

SELF-RECRUITING

One of the most common methods of recruitment is to do it yourself. The DIY method can be slow and draining, and you should plan for extra lead time since your team won't be dedicated to recruitment full-time. Plan for a minimum of two weeks for DIY recruiting, and you may start with a call for participants from colleagues, friends, and family. Still, you should include a screener email or survey to ensure appropriateness. Because of the limited formality, tools like Google Forms can be paired with an introduction email to screen possible recruits (see Figure 7-7).

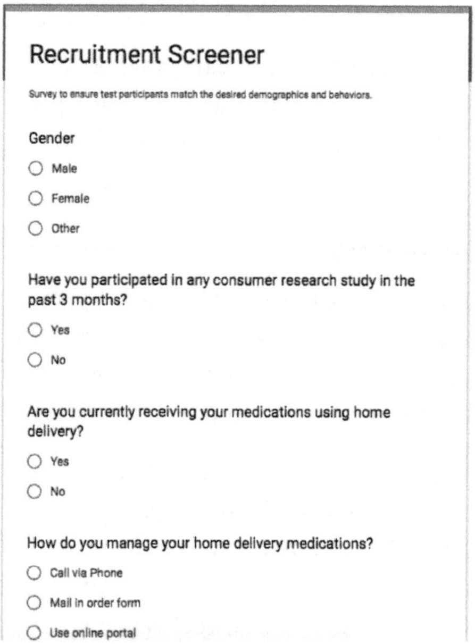

Recruitment Screener

Survey to ensure test participants match the desired demographics and behaviors.

Gender

○ Male

○ Female

○ Other

Have you participated in any consumer research study in the past 3 months?

○ Yes

○ No

Are you currently receiving your medications using home delivery?

○ Yes

○ No

How do you manage your home delivery medications?

○ Call via Phone

○ Mail in order form

○ Use online portal

FIGURE 7-7

A DIY Google Form screener

Cold calling

Cold calling is probably the most uncomfortable recruiting method. This requires access to a list of phone numbers of individuals who have opted in to provide feedback. Numbers may be obtained through an online survey or, in some cases, purchased from companies that specialize in selling customer contact information.

Even when customers agree to being contacted, there can be a moment of confusion as to why you are calling them. To handle this, your opening script should clearly state the reason why you're calling and how you got their number.

In-person intercepts

One recruiting option is to go to where the participants are located (see Figure 7-8). If recruiting participants in situ, you want to go to a high-traffic area where you are likely to have access to people fitting your user profiles. It is important to have a 5- to 10-second elevator pitch of who you are and what you are doing. We highly encourage you to carry a clipboard, as this lends you more credibility when you approach people or when they ask who you are. Don't get discouraged if most people don't seem interested. People live busy lives and in many cases have trained themselves to ignore strangers approaching them to complete some sort of survey.

FIGURE 7-8
Researchers often seek participants in the environment where they are most likely to be found

Online intercepts. People accessing your product online or through a companion website are candidates for participating in user research. For passive analytics, users participate simply by using the site. For more active surveys or unmoderated tests, users may be presented with a pop up asking if they are interested in participating in research activities. This call to action should quickly explain what the activity is and what kind of incentive is available to participants. One of the common tools for doing this type of recruitment is Ethnio, an online screening service (Figure 7-9).

FIGURE 7-9
A screener presented by Ethnio to recruit users for research

Other alternatives. Other ways to recruit include banner ads targeted to visitors to a product's website, or email blasts to users who've agreed to learn about updates. Banner ads are often paid advertisements. Email blasts, on the other hand, obtain a list of potential recruits from marketing departments. These are not great as a primary recruiting approach, but your team can't be recruiting 24/7. By having these passive methods available, you might get a few users that your normal methods might miss.

OUTSOURCING RECRUITING

Recruiting doesn't have to be your team's responsibility. Companies specialize in finding participants on your behalf. In some ways, this is a more effective method. It's important that someone from your team manages and oversees the recruitment efforts, however. This is especially true for client-based recruiting, as detailed next.

Third-party recruiting

Market research firms have perfected the method of finding people that fit into demographically based buckets. These firms take well-written recruitment screeners and call people in their databases for a reasonable fee. While this fee depends on the complexity of your screener, the resulting participants tend to be better than most DIY methods.

Client-based recruiting

For client-based work, it's possible to offload recruiting to members of the client team. This is a good method if recruitment efforts depend on relationships, such as a wealth management tool. Using this method increases the importance of having a team member oversee the recruitment efforts. It's easy for clients to find the most available participant, regardless of appropriateness. This may lead to more junior or less experienced participants, which can bias results.

SCHEDULING

The art of scheduling research participants takes time and patience. Your team will balance the needs of the moderators, observers, and participants. For intensive qualitative research methods, you should aim to schedule only three to four participants a day. For lighter forms of qualitative methods, this increases to five to six participants in a day without exhausting the research team.

Quantitative methods have fewer scheduling constraints, as participants either are unaware of the session through web analytics or access the research tool for a short period of time. For unmoderated research a participant should be able to complete the session in 15–30 minutes. After 30 minutes without a moderator to keep them on task, participants lose focus.

BACKUPS

It is rare that everyone who agrees to participate in a qualitative research activity is able to contribute meaningful information. This is expected, and many teams schedule backup participants in case the scheduled ones don't attend. This is a good practice, no matter the form of research.

No shows

If you have 10 people scheduled for a series of research sessions, you'll be lucky if 8 show up. This doesn't speak to the value of the work your team is doing or the level of interest in your product. Lives and schedules are complicated, and spending an hour with some stranger can easily be deprioritized.

When this happens, backup participants are key to having research data. It's not uncommon to schedule a backup participant across multiple research sessions. The backup waits to be called on if another participant doesn't show up. This way, if the second or third participant doesn't show, the backup may be used. Backups are compensated for their time in similar ways as participants. If you don't have backups, take this time to catch up on work that has built up. If clients are uncomfortable with no shows, explain that this is an unavoidable part of the process.

Duds

No recruitment effort is bulletproof. You will get participants who make you wonder how they made it through the screener. As with no shows, this is part of the process and happens during most research activities. While "duds" may not be perfect participants, they still have something to contribute. You will need to modify your tactics during the session to hyperfocus on key goals, and you'll need to flag any notes from that session as supplemental to your data set. Chapter 10 explores improvisation techniques as a tool for adjusting your approach on the fly in more detail.

Voice from the Streets

Jeremy Canfield,
Service and Experience Designer

How do you approach recruiting participants?

It's hard to overstate the importance of recruiting. It's hard, awkward, and time-consuming, but without it and the users it brings, all other parts of designing a product or service fall back on the internal team's assumptions.

Working on a public works tool, we have a weekly cycle of testing and incorporating the results of the testing into the next sprint's development tasks. This requires a more or less constant flow of users, and the outreach, scheduling, and reminders that recruiting these users necessitates. In order to connect with the users we need, we have used a variety of methods, but our go-to for the weekly testing is the web intercept. Folks browsing the website are presented with a small pop-over that asks if they are interested in participating in making the site better; they can click through to sign up. For the folks who do sign up, we send out an email on Monday asking if they have availability for later that week, and include a self-scheduler that integrates with our calendaring system and allows them to pick a time that works for them. We follow up with connection details (we host the vast majority of our testing remotely) and a reminder the day before.

This process certainly isn't bulletproof: not all of our recruited users show up and we generally don't have enough folks in the queue to maintain backups, meaning we may have to shift the folks who are observing testing to other tasks with little notice. It also relies on a fairly engaged user base being willing to sign up and take time out of their busy schedules, which also means that we sometimes have to make special efforts to find specialized user classes who aren't as well represented in our signups.

That said, this process works pretty well for us because the site's traffic means that we get a fresh set of folks on a weekly basis, and weekly recruiting also gives us quick feedback loops to find out not only what's working with the website, but what messaging is working in recruiting, reminding, and the testing itself: we often end up tweaking the test based on the users who have signed up for spots, and the weekly cycle means that we can revise the tests that didn't fully uncover what we wanted to learn.

Recruitment Challenges

Every recruitment effort has challenges. Some of the most common hurdles aren't challenges, but excuses we tell ourselves to avoid recruiting in the first place. The following scenarios have stopped more research opportunities than any stakeholder claiming insufficient funding.

I DON'T HAVE USERS...YET

Just because the product you are creating isn't on the market today doesn't mean you don't have "users." Your product is trying to solve a problem. Your product has potential competitors and, barring that, analog counterparts. Identify how people work around the existing problem by applying solutions passed down through generations, hacking together fixes, or using another product in an unintended way for a desired outcome. The things people do and how they do them are out there somewhere. Your focus of research should be not the product itself, but the problem your product will solve.

SMALL TARGET AUDIENCE

Some products serve a very niche group of people. This is common for internal products that are used by a well-defined pool of users. Just because a user pool is small, however, doesn't mean it should be a challenge to reach. In fact, it's the opposite. Small user groups are a focused audience. It might take some relationship managing with supervisors or other gatekeepers, but it will pay off in the end. For example, if you need to talk with high-level vice presidents who are in charge of procurement at an organization, your time might be better spent reaching out to their assistants to schedule a meeting rather than contacting the vice presidents directly.

COMMON LIES WE TELL OURSELVES

Without a cohesive screener, product teams often find recruiting challenging. Two of the most common indicators of a loose or undefined screener are "everyone is a user" and "everything is a secret."

Everyone is a user

Simply put, everyone is *not* your user. Even Facebook, which is available to everyone, started with a specific user group: college students. If you are designing for a very large population of people, user groups can subdivide the pool into manageable segments that relate to how, when, and why people might use your product.

Everything is a secret

No team wants word of their product to get out before they are ready to send out a media kit. There are ways to ensure news of your product doesn't go public until you're ready. As mentioned in Chapter 6, your nondisclosure agreements legally silence participants. You can also display prototypes or early releases without naming your company, product, or team.

In reality, the people you recruit are not the type to perform corporate espionage. In fact, they will be honored to be included, and once your product goes live they could be some of your strongest supporters.

Exercise: Priming Your Screener

There is a quick exercise you can conduct with your team to prime your recruitment screener. Together, you will map out what key demographics you want to target and the types of behaviors that you want to observe.

1. **List out basic demographics.**

   List out the basic demographics like age, education, income, family, ethnicity, and employment. Members of the team, on their own, select the demographics they think matter for your product and then share with the group. Based on what the team shares, find the top three to five demographics and write those down for all to see.

2. **Write down desired behaviors.**

   Next, have each person on the team write down the actions or behaviors they would like to learn more about that people do with your product. Once they've listed out their behaviors, have them share them with the group and note any overlaps. Discuss any behaviors that are mentioned once to understand why that person thought it was important to research more about it. Likewise, discussing overlaps uncovers clear gaps in existing knowledge. Once more, pick the top three to five behaviors that the team agrees are the most important to learn more about.

3. **Write screening surveys.**

Once the basic demographics and behavioral demographics are identified, have team members suggest questions and answers to address the behaviors identified in Step 2 that can be used to screen potential participants. The resulting survey will be your draft screener, which you can review and iterate after finishing the group exercise.

Parting Thoughts

Recruitment can be one of the biggest risks you will face. You don't want to get to the end of your research and find out that you didn't collect any information that actually helps your team. This isn't meant to scare you; rather, we want you to understand that recruitment isn't an area you want to skim over when starting research.

We have both been part of research efforts where recruitment was shortchanged. Those experiences have given us the tools we've presented in this chapter so you can avoid the same problems. Remember, at the heart of any good research effort is the collection and communication of information. If you don't use the right sources for that information, then the value of your research is limited.

[*Part III*]

Facilitating Research

THIS PART OF THE BOOK transitions from preparing good questions and planning research to conducting research. While this is often an exciting aspect of research, proper preparations and situational awareness often go hand in hand with the most effective research initiatives.

Making Research Happen
> At its core, research requires practice and rehearsal. Chapter 8 will apply the logistics outlined earlier in a more how-to manner as you sit down with stakeholders and customers alike.

Managing People During Research
> Just as stretching before exercising is helpful, any good research initiative starts with a warm-up exercise. This allows the designers to adjust to the researcher mindset and allows participants to get comfortable with the tasks and conversations they've agreed to be part of. Chapter 9 will walk you through this process.

Improv in Research
> The best-laid research plans often have at least one unexpected surprise. Chapter 10 will identify ways to pivot when you face common hurdles such as technical issues, personality challenges, or a sudden shift in expectations.

Facilitating Research
> At its core, all research studies human behavior. Chapter 11 will look at some of the softer skills invaluable in being respectful and effective as product designers.

Debrief Sessions

Nobody has perfect memory. And just as analysis and reporting are important, so are more immediate and frequent debrief sessions. Chapter 12, the final chapter in this part of the book, will provide a structure of when, where, and how to effectively conduct internal debriefing sessions.

Making Research Happen

The Code is more of what you'd call "guidelines" than actual rules.
—CAPTAIN BARBOSSA, *PIRATES OF THE CARIBBEAN*

Crafting good questions is key to any research initiative. Choosing methods and coordinating logistics is critical to ensure appropriate expectations are set within a project team. At the end of the day, though, none of this matters if the research itself fails to execute on its mission. This chapter explores the tactical side of performing research, including team roles and how to use many of the documents outlined in Chapter 6.

Rules of Engagement

Rules govern human behavior. Whether this is in regards to sports, board games, family dynamics, or company hierarchy, a set of guiding principles defines our roles and interactions with one another. Research is no different. We refer to these tactics as "rules," though we urge you to think of them more as "guidelines," as Captain Barbossa famously said in *Pirates of the Caribbean* (2003).

DEFINING YOUR ROLES

Moderator and note taker

The best research initiatives have two key roles: a moderator and a note taker. While many aspects of research are adjusted for scope and budget, this is one rule that should be nonnegotiable. Qualitative research is an intensive process, and having the support of a team member is imperative to maintaining flow and pace throughout days of research.

While quantitative research tends to be more analytical and metric focused, the second set of eyes is still paramount in establishing good research practices and ensuring a well-rounded view of the data.

Moderator

The moderator is the game-show host of a session. For quantitative research, this may be the person who coordinates and defines scripts for gathering or organizing data. In a qualitative study, this is the main point of contact for participants. The moderator handles all participant engagement from the time they walk through the door of the lab to the time they leave with their honorarium.

A moderator's role is to guide the conversation. With the support of the discussion guide, moderators move from one task to the next and look to probe where interesting or unexpected behaviors arise.

The moderator should not be responsible for notes and capturing the session! While it is possible for individuals to actively listen and take notes, or actively listen and formulate a response, it is very difficult to do all three at the same time. Even more so, taking notes requires a level of disengagement from the participant, and the moderator's role is to be actively engaged with the study at all times.

Note taker

While the moderator quarterbacks the discussion, the note taker helps capture the key information. Armed with the same discussion guide and familiarity with the system as the moderator, the note taker captures and organizes observations for later study.

While it is not critical that note takers have a background in research methods, it is often helpful to discuss the goals of the research and level of detail desired in notes before a session.

Even in quantitative research, note takers play a key role of tracking and maintaining data, while the moderator often looks at broader, more strategic implications.

Almost as important as having the moderator and note taker roles is an understanding of who on your team will be responsible for each role. Roles can change too. The moderator for one session doesn't need to be the moderator for every session. In fact, there is something to be gained by changing roles between sessions. This allows everyone trained in conducting research to probe for information and offers mental respite to moderators and note takers alike.

Remember, research is based on discussion guides and specific goals, so while the voice of the researcher may change, the overall flow goals will remain consistent. What is most critical is to ensure that everyone on the team is aware of and comfortable with their roles in a given session so that the research team presents an air of confidence, professionalism, and ease.

Teacher and student

While a research team takes two, it is important not to discount the participant's role. The participant ultimately leads the conversation, with guidance from the moderator's discussion guide. The participant chooses what to share and what to hold back.

The best research sessions start by setting the expectation that the researchers are here to learn from the participant. A common way of doing this is to describe the session as a teacher and student relationship rather than an interviewer and interviewee. In this way, the fact that the moderator may ask probing questions to learn more about the participant's work is understood from the get-go.

OBSERVING RESEARCH

So far we have discussed the roles of research as a moderator and a note taker. We strongly urge that you not overwhelm participants with more than two people in their personal space and, fortunately, technology facilitates this by allowing remote observation.

More formal settings, such as usability labs, may have an observation room separated by one-way glass (see Figure 8-1). With the use of screen-sharing services, observers may be able to dial in to listen and observe a session from a building, city, or country away.

In either case, observers are a key part of any research project. As part of the product team, they provide a way to streamline synthesis and the communication of findings. Business stakeholders are often more engaged and open to findings when they're able to observe challenges and opportunities themselves. At the end of the day, you can never have too many observers, so we encourage you to invite all stakeholders to participate in the observation process. Again, though, we caution you about how many observers have direct interaction with the participant. You want to encourage a feeling of trust and conversation and, more importantly, ensure that the participant doesn't feel like a specimen on display in a lab. The more personal an interaction, the better.

FIGURE 8-1
Observation labs have many shapes and forms, though a common element is one-way glass to observe participants in an unobtrusive manner

Observer role

In anthropology, observers often try to be as unobtrusive as possible. While this is true with product research as well, observers can also offer additional insights and opportunities to probe.

It is common practice, especially with qualitative research, to step away from participants near the end of a session to check with observers, either behind the glass or through remote means, to see if they have any additional questions not covered by the session.

Ground rules

As with the moderator and note taker roles, setting expectations for the observer role is important. Some common rules for observers include providing:

- A disclaimer that, while the session will follow the discussion guide for the study as closely as possible, it may—due to the nature of qualitative research—go in a different order or explore tasks not immediately documented

- A request for observers to write down questions as they occur

- A guideline that observers will not interrupt the session during the flow

- An opportunity to discuss questions observers identify during the session before the participant leaves

- A request that observers take notes on the provided notepads and write down any quotes that stand out or interactions they found insightful.

Dry Runs

As mentioned in Chapter 2, dry runs are the dress rehearsal of product research. If this is a quantitative study, ensure that any scripts work on a production or QA environment before pushing them to the live product. Even better, once those scripts are pushed, have a few colleagues test the workflow and confirm that data is being appropriately captured.

For qualitative studies, dry runs are even more critical. Practice sessions allow moderators, note takers, and observers alike to get accustomed to the cadence and flow of a session. If a task is ordered poorly or missing context, now is the time to resolve this.

A common question regarding rehearsing research is "How?" Dry runs do not need to be done with actual participants. Often product teams will recruit colleagues who might not be intimately familiar with the research goals and will ask them to act as participants. The goals are to check technology, flow, and resources, not gather usable data.

PRACTICE MAKES PERFECT

Just as in any presentation, the more you practice, the higher your chances of success. This includes reading the script out loud to be comfortable with the dialogue and clicking through the prototype to understand where the challenges and hiccups are.

EMBRACE CHANGE

Change is good. And there is no time to change like practice sessions. While it is possible to adjust a research protocol after visiting with a few participants, it is highly encouraged that you be as consistent as possible within a session's parameters. This is especially true with quantitative measures to ensure you're comparing "apples to apples."

One goal of practice sessions is to determine if the right questions are being asked in the right way—if questions are being posed in the right order or with the best intent, for example. Dry runs are the last stage before participants are brought in for task analysis, and it is never too late to make adjustments to discussion guides and workflows (resources permitting).

Session Flow and Facilitating

In Chapter 6, we presented many artifacts that come with research: welcome kits, discussion guides, consent forms, and honorariums. In this section we will discuss how these are used in the context of research. While these are written in the context of moderated qualitative methods, many remote practices and quantitative research that requires active participant engagement (such as diary studies) may also require these tools.

ADDRESS THE FORMALITIES FIRST

Shortly after a participant is shown to a research lab, or the research team arrives at their destination, the consent forms and honorariums should be addressed. While this seems draconian, getting these out of the way addresses any legal implications and sets a formal tone.

Consent forms

As discussed in Chapter 6, consent forms may include nondisclosure agreements, permission to record, and permissions to quote participants. Two copies of each document should be made for each session, one for the product team to file and another for the participant to keep.

Honorariums

Honorariums should be addressed at the beginning of a session, though it is common to actually provide the honorarium after any closing discussion. Make clear that the honorarium is in recognition of the participant's time today, and that if they feel uncomfortable or are unable to continue a task, the honorarium is theirs regardless.

Voice from the Streets

Emma Lawler, Product Designer

In a few words, describe your job.

I create the user experience and interfaces for a fitness workout application on iPhone, Android, and wearable devices.

How do you approach research for physical products?

When setting up a space for a user test, we make sure the participant feels like they are in a private space where other people are not directly watching them. We set up two conference rooms—one for the user and the moderator to interact in, and another for viewers of the study to watch the live video. There is a webcam connected to Google Hangouts in the testing room, and a live stream of the video to the observation room. Even though the user knows they are being filmed, it's important they feel comfortable enough to exercise and use the product. Doing downward dog or side lunges for the first time can make people feel a little uncomfortable.

The moderator is the person who sets up the entire test environment for the user. We make sure to have the same person welcoming participants to the location, setting up the study, and walking them through their tasks. The main role of the moderator is to make the participant feel comfortable so they talk through what they're doing, and how they feel.

The note taker is in the observation room, watching and listening to take notes on key parts of the test. We create a Google spreadsheet ahead of time so there is a structure to the note taking. If we know the user will be doing an exercise prompted on screen, we'll have a column for their perceived understanding of the prompt, and a column for whether or not they actually do the move correctly. The moderator should also ask the participant about how they feel at key points in the test to get quotes and insights the user might be thinking to themselves.

Oftentimes the user will look to the moderator for guidance on how to do something, especially when doing physical activity. The moderator can help the user to keep moving forward through the prototype, but should not guide them in a certain direction.

We wrap up by asking the user how they felt overall about the experience, and make sure they leave feeling good about what they completed. The user is never wrong, so it's important to find out what they do or don't understand from the design.

START SLOW

Product research is hard. And if it is difficult for product teams who rehearse and practice a session before meeting with a participant, think of how it must feel to be on the receiving end of these questions. Thus, it is important in any research session to start slow.

After the necessary consent forms and honorarium paperwork is out of the way, research initiatives start with the discussion guide introduction. It is common practice for researchers to read from a script at this point, as mentioned in Chapter 6, and to identify their actions as such. In this way, the participant can ease into the premise of being "on display."

While a discussion guide outline was provided in Chapter 6, the main themes can be summarized in this sample introduction:

> Now that we have covered the paperwork for the session, we would like to begin our research. I am going to read the next section from a script to ensure I don't miss anything, but the rest of our session I would like to treat as an ongoing dialogue where I can get a better understanding of how you go about [specific task].

From there, you can describe the session goals and gather any general information such as interests, familiarity with tech, and so on.

BUILD TO COMPLEXITY

The introduction and demographic information is a great way to ease into any research, be it quantitative or qualitative. Eager to get to the actual conversation, you might be tempted to jump right to the complex questions. It is better to start with simpler, more established tasks and work your way to the more challenging questions. Think of the conversation as a story. You don't start with the big dramatic reveal but build up to it over time.

A common model for this is how video games treat game and level design (Figure 8-2). Levels don't start with the big boss, or big challenges, but with simple, smaller baddies. As the game progresses, the challenges increase, with pauses after big problems for a break or ease in the tension. The goal is to find a balance between personal and complex questions and more in-depth discussions. As the conversation progresses, so does the richness of information.

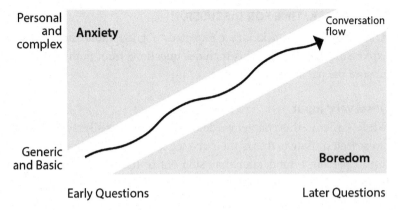

FIGURE 8-2

The game complexity arc illustrates a common way to approach question complexity in interviews

Main tasks

The game complexity arc is best used in context of the main research tasks. This may be as few as two or three tasks or as many as six to eight. The flow allows for a natural and ongoing cadence to the conversation.

While there is no hard and fast number of tasks or duration, it is common practice for moderated sessions to last anywhere from 60 to 90 minutes total and unmoderated sessions to last 15 to 30 minutes. Quantitative studies (such as surveys) should take less than 10 minutes, and more anthropological studies (such as diary studies) should not take more than a few minutes at any one time to respond.

Failure is okay

All participants will not complete all tasks—and this is okay. Part of the introduction should reinforce with participants that the product is being evaluated, not their own skills or intelligence.

With that said, good moderators will prime a participant that they may not offer support immediately in order to preserve the efficacy of the study. At the same time, the moderator should judge when to provide support or move past a task for the sake of the research and the participant's morale alike.

COFFEE TALK: TIME FOR DISCUSSION

After the defined tasks are completed, a good moderator looks to explore any loose ends. This includes questions from both the observers and the participant.

Observers' input

While earlier in this chapter we defined observers as silent members of a research initiative, this is their chance to speak up. If they're observing in person, a moderator may step out of the room to confer with them and gather any outstanding questions, often written on sticky notes for easy transfer.

For remote observers, the note taker may check the communication log from the screen-sharing service to coordinate any questions.

In quantitative research this step may be the occasional check-in with the data and making any necessary adjustments.

Participants' input

Research participants just shared with you their time and, depending on the scope of the research, personal goals or behaviors. It is only courteous to ask them if there is anything they would like to share or if they have any questions about the process as a whole. An added benefit is the participant may really open up about a service. In the instance of evaluating existing products, complaints or opportunities that were not a focus of the research may come to light, opening up avenues for further investigation.

ENDING A SESSION

After the tasks are performed, and questions and answers have made their rounds, thank participants for their time. Providing them with a means to contact your company or recruiting agency if they have any questions is a good way to build rapport and trust should any issues with the honorarium arise.

For sessions where you invite participants to your office, check that logistics (like parking validation) are addressed. Likewise, if you have visited a participant in their workspace, be respectful of their time and place of business and do not linger; more on that in the next chapter.

Exercise: Meeting Prep

Have you ever attended a meeting with your team and experienced technology issues? What about a client presentation where you weren't sure who was presenting or what the rationale was behind a design or business decision? Some of the best products and designs can falter because of poor planning and communication.

For your next internal meeting, take 10 minutes beforehand to make sure your technology works. If you've been at meetings without an agenda, take the time to list out the goals for the session. Take notes as to how the 10 minutes of preparation and testing helps or hinders the meetings. Then do this again with client and stakeholder meetings.

Parting Thoughts

Having gotten this far in the book you may be thinking, "Wow! Research is hard and there is a lot I need to remember!" Fear not, though. No product researcher became an expert in a day. We have all had our share of blunders and missteps about the discussion guide, recruiting, paperwork, and the like.

Research is full of surprises and sudden changes, and even the most seasoned designers need to think on their feet. All we can suggest is go out there to try, and be willing to fail. Not only that, but *look forward to and welcome* failure. From challenges often come our most valuable lessons and, surprisingly, the most usable data. Our next chapter looks at how improv techniques can help us achieve success in research.

[9]

Managing People During Research

Don't shift your weight, look always at your mark but don't stare,
be specific but not memorable, be funny but don't make him laugh.
He's got to like you, then forget you the moment you've left his side.
—RUSTY, OCEAN'S ELEVEN

The elements of a research initiative vary based on scope and type. This makes research seem hard. Fortunately, one common element across any quantitative or qualitative research is you and your team. While you may not be able to control environment or participant engagement, your practice and awareness of social graces can help research feel natural. This chapter looks at some of the softer skills that make research look more natural to participants and stakeholders alike. These skills are not meant to be prescriptive, and vary by culture and environment. We will spend some time exploring the most common interactions.

Host and Guest Norms

For any research where you interact directly with people, it is important to understand and respond appropriately to social or professional cues. This conveys a level of respect that leads to a more natural discussion with participants. One common analogy of this dynamic is the relationship between actors on a stage and the audience. The audience is aware that actors are reading from a script, performing a fictional or historical scene, and transporting the viewer to another place. But through suspension of disbelief and the skill of the actors, the audience is absorbed in the environment rather than set outside of it. Research is the same way. Often described as the "Wizard of Oz technique" because researchers pull the strings behind a literal or figurative curtain, research is about interacting with participants in a seemingly natural way, regardless of the actual behind-the-scenes impact.

DRESS APPROPRIATELY FOR OFFICE VISITS

When you are visiting office settings, it is a good idea to ask your business stakeholders about dress code and office practices. Even if you always visit your client in a suit and tie, asking this question is critical. On many occasions we have been asked to remove our neckties or leave our jackets behind so that employees don't mistake us as managers, or worse, an internal audit team.

Equally important is being dressed for the specific environment. The attire in a medical center is drastically different than that of a construction site. It is not unheard of for researchers shifting between different projects to have to change quickly between sessions, like Clark Kent/ Superman in the phone booth.

BE A GRACIOUS GUEST DURING HOME VISITS

Home visits are measurably more challenging than office visits, as an individual is inviting you into their personal space. While it may feel awkward, take cues from your environment. If you see a line of shoes along the door, ask your host if you should remove your own.

At the same time, when a participant agrees to meet you in their home, they often feel the social pressure of hosting you. To balance social graces with the level of propriety desired of research, we recommend accepting a glass of water (assuming it is offered). You do not need to drink the water, but by merely accepting it you are fitting an expected social interaction and putting your participant at ease.

RESPECT PARTICIPANTS' PERSONAL SPACE

Whether you are meeting at a participant's place of work or in their home, it is important to not be in their personal space for too long. This applies to both before and after a research session.

Don't arrive too early

While it is strongly encouraged that you arrive early to research sessions and ensure that all systems work, do not do this at the participant's desk. Find a coffee shop around the corner, or on another floor of the building, and set up as much of the testing environment as possible.

While it feels cumbersome, walking through the halls of an office with an open laptop connected to a screen-sharing device is preferable to losing the first 10 minutes of a research session to technical issues.

Leave no trace behind

Just as setup for a session should not take place in a participant's personal space, neither should the breakdown after a session. While this is important in office settings, it's critical with home visits. After thanking participants for their time, pack up as efficiently as you can.

Then, almost just as importantly, don't sit in your car in the participant's driveway, or linger outside their office door. Take the extra five minutes to drive around the block or, even better, to a local coffee shop. At this point, take the time needed to sort papers, reset any technology, save files, and prepare for the next session.

FOLLOW SCREEN-SHARING BEST PRACTICES

Remote sessions are easier in the sense that personal space is not a factor. Still, it is important to follow certain social norms. If you're sharing the participant's screen, warn them that anything on their screen will be visible to the observers. This includes the tasks being explored but also anything on the participant's desktop. We have inadvertently seen personal or racy content on participants' screens more times than we care to admit.

If the warning wasn't enough and something unsavory or unprofessional comes across the screen, the best course of action is to try to ignore it. If the problem persists or is distracting, don't be afraid to use technical challenges as an excuse and ask the participant to close other applications in order to avoid "overwhelming the testing tool."

Cultural Considerations

Just as important as host and guest norms are more subtle cultural norms. Research spans the globe, and thus requires awareness and sensitivity to how guests, greetings, and information are exchanged.

Cultural considerations may be as subtle as the definition of personal space but also include conversational cues or body language. While this book cannot go into detail on every variation, we strongly encourage discussing with business stakeholders any cultural or social norms when you're visiting international research locations.

SET THE RIGHT TONE

We speak differently to our colleagues than we do our managers. We have different inflections when discussing life and work with significant others than with parents and friends. With this in mind, the tone you have with research participants sets the baseline for your relationship with them throughout the research session.

All too commonly, an employee learns they are being used in a research study and internally hears, *the company wants to find a way to remove my position.* It is also common that they see researchers as an extension of management.

An easy way to alleviate any concerns about job security is to frame your role as researcher like so: "I'm here to make your job easier by understanding how you approach your work. This may include frustrations or workarounds you've uncovered. Rest assured that while we are recording, our aim is to keep your information as anonymous as possible and we can go 'off the record' any time you feel it's necessary."

KNOW WHEN TO CALL "SCENE"

In improv, a scene is considered complete when one of the actors calls "Scene!" during the performance. While Chapter 10 explores in depth some improvisational techniques as a tool for research, you can't literally shout "Scene!" or "Done!" in front of a research participant. Still, it is important to infer when a participant is finished providing information on a given topic or with the research session altogether. While research often employs the laddering method to probe on the "why" of a task, a good researcher knows how to stop just short of pushing too far.

You might define "done" for a participant when they're giving you the same answer two times in a row, or changing from thorough explanations to one-word answers. Be sensitive to how your participants respond to your cues. It is very difficult to gain someone's trust and comfort once the cadence and ease of a conversation is lost.

Voice from the Streets

Lis Hubert

The often-overlooked, but vitally important, participant warm-up part of any session is actually the part that I look forward to the most. Why? Because it is during this time that I'm able to gauge where a participant is at, and adjust my approach to match. My research and observation senses are primed and ready, and my facilitation and communication senses kick into gear.

In order to find this alignment, for each session, I usually start by warming up myself. I start with a mental warm-up by closing my eyes for a few moments, clearing my head, and then reminding myself of the recruitment data for the person I'm about to talk to. I also work to remember that the next hour is not about me, but about someone else completely.

I then warm up my body by making sure I've gotten up and walked a little, rolled my neck a few times or stretched my arms...whatever I can do to reset my muscles to prepare them for a new person.

Once the participant has arrived (either in person, or on the other end of a call), I go through my checklist of logistics comments and questions, and then I ask them the all-important, "OK, so tell me about yourself. In regards to <topic we are discussing> what is your role or how do you relate?" As I listen to their response, I create a mental map of the participant. I note their communication style, any word preferences, their posture. Then I immediately meet them where they are by mimicking and mirroring their characteristics back to them.

That's really it, and it hardly ever fails. Within those first two to three minutes, I almost always see or hear even the most shy or guarded participant jovially and happily engaged in the session.

Small Talk Matters

A lot of this chapter circles around the idea of small talk. While one aspect of this is filling gaps in conversation and recognizing an individual's comfort level, another aspect is having a respectful tone of voice.

In the medical world, this is referred to as "bedside manner" and refers to the doctor's tone and attitude toward a patient. In the research world, it translates to treating participants with respect and establishing a strong teacher and apprentice role, where they can guide you as the researcher through their experiences.

PRIMING QUESTIONS

Small talk is a learned skill. The easiest way to practice it is to use priming questions. These include demographic questions including age, profession, and familiarity with a product or toolkit. Small talk goes beyond that, though, and offers a more conversational tone to the session. Don't be afraid to offer some of your own personal information, as it may help open your participant up to the discussion. Be careful, though. This is not a friend or colleague you are meeting with but a research participant. While sharing personal information is appropriate, always make sure you are maintaining an appropriate level of professionalism and not marring the data collected.

TAKING NOTES

We already discussed the role of the moderator and the note taker, but we did not focus on how notes are captured. Since we want to focus on human conversations, it is important to have a system that is as unobtrusive as possible. The two options for capturing notes are straightforward: pen and paper or on a computer. While there is no right answer for one or the other, there are considerations for each.

Pen and paper

Pen and paper offers the ease and efficiency of going where you go, not being tied down to an outlet, and being unobtrusive. Taking notes on a legal pad or directly on a copy of the discussion guide is an easy way to naturally capture information in the context of the session.

Some drawbacks to pen and paper are around sharing. You need to scan, photograph, or transcribe your notes before they can be distributed. This leads to a bigger concern if you cannot read your shorthand after the fact. We prefer handwritten notes, and have developed our own shorthand that we then transcribe into a digital tool as soon as possible after a session.

Digital notes
Digital notes work too and offer you the option to immediately share and distribute notes. A number of tools pair digital audio recording with typed notes, providing more context to what was said.

One important consideration for digital notes is the cadence of your typing. As you start and stop writing, a participant can easily ignore (if they even hear) the scratch of your pen on paper. The clicking of keys, however, can make a participant self-conscious about what they are saying and how you are reacting. If digital note taking is your preferred method, we suggest finding a consistent cadence so it seems as if you never stop typing—even if this means typing "the quick brown fox jumped over the lazy dog" as you wait for feedback. This allows the sound of the keyboard to fall into the background so the participant isn't distracted by your note taking.

WARMING UP
Warming up, whether it is the oven before cooking or your muscles before playing sports, is critical. Research is no different. We refer to warming up as the softer side of research because the transition from practice to research often happens seamlessly and, depending on the scale of the research, may require us to revisit these exercises throughout a session.

Still, research hinges on warming up. Think for a moment how a participant would behave if you walked into a room and immediately started asking them personal financial or health-related information? These are sensitive topics, and balancing the rich data with the appropriate level of humanity and empathy is key to gathering good data. In longer interviews and discussions, taking breaks from the script to hear a tangential story allows participants to open up and is just as valuable as their insights to product design.

Soft skills and warming up aren't exclusive to the beginning of a session. Near the close of sessions it is not uncommon to circle back to more social discussions. In this way, the personal "meat" of a discussion is sandwiched between softer, more lightweight questions. This can go a long way in leaving a participant feeling heard and respected, and with positive feelings toward your product and research team.

Exercises: Making Small Talk

Small talk, or warming up, is a soft skill that's not easily taught and requires active practice. While this book will not make you an expert in small talk, the following exercise takes less than five minutes a day and can help you become more comfortable in these social situations.

OFFICE SMALL TALK

Take a mental audit of your coworkers. Who do you talk to on a regular basis? Who might you know in passing but have not built a relationship with? Focus on the second list and, once a day (or once a week), make an effort to strike up a conversation with them. This doesn't have to be anything overly personal or awkward, but as you cross paths in the mailroom or kitchen, rather than simply saying hello ask what projects they are working on, how they like the new office renovations, or how they fared during the last snowstorm. Make a concerted effort to change whom you speak with each day and cycle back on the colleagues you spoke with early on. Who knows, an added benefit could be some stronger office relationships too.

COFFEE TALK

If you work in a small office, or would rather practice with total strangers, think of the coffee shop you frequent. Do you simply pay your barista and go on your way? Do you stand in line staring at your phone? Instead of doing that, strike up a conversation with the clerk or other patrons. We don't mean that you should pry, but using simple icebreakers like "I hope the seasonal latte comes back soon" will build your confidence in having conversations with people you don't know well.

Parting Thoughts

An entire book could be spent on soft skills in kicking off research. We have personally experienced the various graces and blunders outlined in this chapter. While the ones covered here are important, all researchers come up with their own methods to handle social graces in a research and product setting. The important thing is that you don't lose sight of the personal touches that make people comfortable in a research session.

To become comfortable with your own approach, start by imitating your mentors. From there, you can find your voice and make research your own. This ownership and personalization is critical to being true to your goals and comfortable in your own skin. The following chapter focuses on ways to shift and pivot during research to build your own research persona.

Improv in Research

The best-laid plans of mice and men, often go awry.
—ADAPTED FROM ROBERT BURNS, "TO A MOUSE"

Humans are fickle. And no amount of planning, preparation, or experience can mitigate every possible variable. While we've encouraged testing technology, recruiting backups, and other methods to support an efficient research process, things ultimately don't go as planned. Improvisational techniques are an invaluable way to approach the unknown with a positive outlook. This chapter introduces improv techniques and shares their application to research and product design as a whole.

What Is Improv?

Improv is storytelling. In traditional terms, it is simply telling a story you haven't written down. This doesn't have to be a complex story. In fact, recounting how your day went or describing your plans for tomorrow are perfect examples of improvising stories. In the professional setting, storytelling and research are very much aligned. We craft questions for stakeholders and participants but have no idea what responses we may get. Improv gives researchers the ability to think on our feet and pivot at a moment's notice based on the reactions and feedback we receive.

IMPROV FOR THE MASSES

While improv is not specific to comedy, we often associate one with the other. Second City, Saturday Night Live, and Monty Python's Flying Circus are all examples of popular improv troupes. You may have attended an open-mic night at a local comedy venue where improv games were showcased (see Figure 10-1). Toastmasters, an organization for improving public speaking, also employs improv techniques as a way for people to gain comfort and skill while giving public addresses. Improv is often enjoyable to watch and to participate in. You may be asking how improv techniques apply to our work as product designers.

FIGURE 10-1
Traditional improv troupe on stage

Rules of Improv

Before we talk about improv as part of product design and product research, it is important to understand the fundamentals of improvisational theater. There are as many rules of improv as there are improv troupes. The 10 rules outlined next were selected because they have direct application to design and research. Each rule is accompanied by an improv game or technique you can use to practice that idea.

EVERYTHING IS TRUE

One of the universal truths of improv is that everything is true. In improv we call this *acceptance*. If a player states they are tired, excited, or acting as a giraffe, then it is true. This aligns to design brainstorming sessions where there is no such thing as a bad idea and all feedback is welcome.

In research, it is important to remember that everything a participant says is, to them, true. It is important not to correct what a participant says or to try to change their behavior. Correcting a participant breaks the teacher–student model and can put a participant on the defensive. Instead of correcting a participant, make a note that a data point should be validated later with stakeholders or other participants.

"Yes, And..."

As discussed in Chapter 2, laddering is a technique where we ask participants "why?" to gain a richer understanding of their world. "Yes, And..." is an improv game and research mindset that practices this technique (Figure 10-2). To play, gather a group of two to five players. After choosing a scene or location, start a conversation with your counterparts. Each response should start with "Yes, and..." where the scale of the story is always increased. For instance, if the first phrase is "Do you want to go to the beach?" the response could be "Yes, and let's take the invisible jet!"

FIGURE 10-2
Design workshop playing "Yes, And..."

STOP TRYING TO BE FUNNY

A common misconception about improv is that you have to be funny. Improv is about storytelling, communicating, and connecting with an audience. Just as creativity doesn't happen on a whim, funny is a muscle that must be exercised and practiced.

In research, it is important to remember that participants are human and that rich data points or sound bytes can't be forced. Improv skills help you facilitate an engaging conversation with participants, allowing interesting data points to naturally develop.

Five-Word Warm-Up

A common method of warming up before an improv show is to stand in a circle with your teammates and shout out short (five words or fewer), random statements. These don't need to make sense, or even be complete thoughts. They may be as concise as "The T-Rex is loose" or as unstructured as "bippity-biminy-bop!" The point is not to be funny, but to get used to saying the first thing that comes to mind. Likewise, when preparing to kick off research, it is not uncommon for teams to play rapid-fire Q&A to get in the mindset of reacting to their surroundings. While these questions and answers should be framed around the project, they don't need to be complex or thorough. Asking "Why is the user here?" followed by "What are Terms and Conditions?" can jumpstart your brain in reacting to and thinking about possible behaviors.

FAILURE IS OK

As with any creative process, we fail in improv more than we succeed. The question is not if we will fail, but how we respond when we do. As discussed, not all research initiatives or sessions are successes, and it is in our best interest to support one another when we struggle. Failure in improv is straightforward—no laughs or not telling a clear story. In research, failure may be technical issues with a prototype, a dud participant, or simply having an "off" day.

Only Questions

One of the most difficult improv games for us is called Only Questions (Figure 10-3). In it, two players act out a scene, talking to each other using only questions. This is a great opportunity for researchers to find questions out of existing information and to seek a richer understanding of their subject. If you struggle with this game as much as we do, it is also a humbling experience that makes failure in the professional realm more approachable.

FIGURE 10-3
Design workshop with two lines of participants playing Only Questions

LISTEN TO THE SCENE

A common challenge new improv artists face is trying to think of their next line. There is a desire to be clever, witty, and funny. But, as mentioned, the goal of improv is not to be funny, and it is OK to fail. One way to avoid these pitfalls is to actively listen to the scene.

In research, this is often described as *active listening*. What is your participant saying and what are they leaving unsaid? By focusing on what you are hearing and using the discussion guide flexibly to hit milestones, you can make necessary adjustments to have a more engaging conversation and uncover richer feedback. This doesn't mean you should throw the script away entirely, but each conversation is unique and requires minor adjustments in real time to account for the human element.

Dinner Party

Dinner Party (Figure 10-4) is an improv game where a single player acts as "host" for three to five other improv "guests." The guests each portray a specific character or trait. This could be a historical person such as Abe Lincoln, a celebrity like Kim Kardashian, or a stereotype like a mime. The key is that while the audience and guests know their roles, the host does not. As the skit is played out, the host must guess their guests' identity based solely on their behavior. This game requires a large degree of active listening and awareness and can directly inform behavior in a research session.

FIGURE 10-4
Design workshop with participants playing Dinner Party including "guests" acting as *Pokémon Go* players and a Gatsby elite

SUPPORT YOUR PLAYERS

Improv, like research, is not a lone task. In improv it is common for players to support one another as a story evolves to allow everyone stage time and to avoid burnout. In research, support may be as subtle as the balance between the moderator and note taker roles, or as direct as changing responsibilities between sessions to avoid mental fatigue. In both improv and research, the focus should be on making your team-mates' skills shine, and relieving strain if a session or activity becomes stressful for them.

Evil Twin

Played with four people, Evil Twin (Figure 10-5) starts with two actors performing a scene. At any point, one of the other two players can yell "Freeze!" At this point they will tap out a player and the scene will continue. The catch is that the new actor will perform as the original's "evil twin." After a few moments a player can call "Freeze!" again, at which point the original twin returns to the scene and has to rationalize, fix, or adjust based on the damage done by their evil twin.

FIGURE 10-5
Design workshop playing Evil Twin, set at the beach; in this case, the evil twin destroyed imaginary sand castles

LOCATION, LOCATION, LOCATION

In theater and performances it is important to set the scene, the location, and the time period. In research, it is important to know who our users are, where they are using our product, and in what channels they may be accessing our service. While this seems obvious, not answering these questions can lead to a lot of the challenges that discussion guides, recruitment screeners, and test plans aim to mitigate. Fortunately, Chapters 6 through 9 offer resources on creating these artifacts. Improv offers other ways to explore these questions.

Bodystorming

Bodystorming (Figure 10-6) is an improv game where a prop (a bicycle helmet, a large foam die, or anything in between) is used to explore a new product or solution. For this game, a team of three to five actors are assigned roles specific to a problem or scene. They then make up ways the prop can solve the problem. The goal isn't to come up with practical solutions but to see how analog objects can inform the creative process through nonlinear thinking.

FIGURE 10-6
Design workshop bodystorming new electronic health record behaviors with a plush fish toy

RAISE THE STAKES

This rule is very similar to the "everything is true" rule covered earlier. It is important in improv to always raise the stakes. For instance, if a skit is taking place on a boat, why not make it the *Titanic*? If the scene is a road trip with a group of friends, why not run out of gas in the desert?

In research, it is important to think of how a problem may be larger than it appears. If you are designing an application for contacting road-side assistance to change a flat tire, are you crafting the story around an easy case, like the car being in the driveway? If so, can you raise the stakes and set the location to the freeway? The latter involves a level of drama and risk that can help expose unknown or hidden design opportunities.

I'd Rather Not

Where "Yes, And..." is a game of agreeing and pivoting, "I'd Rather Not" focuses on denial and offering countersolutions. Take this game at face value; it is one of the few times denial is encouraged in improv. The rules are simple: two players have a conversation and each response starts with, "I'd rather not, why don't we...?" The idea is to take a small idea and come back with a larger one.

YIELD TO THE STRONGEST OFFER

On the coattails of raising the stakes, yielding to the strongest offer means agreeing and supporting our fellow improv actors in creating the strongest scene. Our goal is to create successful products and inform compelling stories. The easiest way to do that is to take the best ideas from everyone involved. Whether in improv or product design, being willing to see a strong idea for what it is leads to success.

In research as well as design feedback, this rule may mean responding to a stakeholder's feedback or a participant's idea and evolving it into something more refined for testing and further validation.

Slide Show

While slide projectors are a relic of the past, sharing vacation photos is timeless and universal. Slide Show (Figure 10-7) is a game where one player acts as the storyteller and the other actors (three to five) act as their family and friends in the photos. Usually the troupe begins by asking for story ideas from the audience. Then the narrator describes the selected story, and the other actors act out the scene in a series of stills. The "image" changes when the narrator makes a clicking noise. The players in the slides support the storyteller in the clues he gives, and the storyteller likewise reacts to the positions of his fellow actors.

FIGURE 10-7

Design workshop playing Slide Show, acting out a member's first date

YOU ARE NOT THE STAR

It is common to think of performers as the "star of the show." In acting, and especially in improv, it is important to check ego at the door. You are not the star of a performance.

In product research, you are also not the star. The star is the story, product, and audience. Your performance is secondary to how you craft a compelling narrative and invite the audience to join you on your journey. Chapter 14 goes into more detail in crafting a story arc for presentations.

In research, the product you are designing is important, but understanding your customers' needs and your stakeholders' concerns is critical. A good researcher understands these needs and looks forward to having their hypothesis and ideas proven wrong in support of more creative, bigger ideas that address a product's needs beyond what they could have considered individually.

Sit-Stand-Lean

Sit-Stand-Lean is played in groups of three. You pick a scene or activity—for instance, folding laundry. Throughout the scene, one player must always be sitting, one standing, and one leaning. Try to change positions during the skit, while watching your fellow players. Since you are not the star, you want to build up what others are saying and doing so that your position supports the scene and story.

REMEMBER EVERYTHING

A common way to end an improv sketch is through *reincorporation*; that is, something mentioned at the start of a skit may be mentioned again at the closing as a way to come full circle and end the scene. While this doesn't translate the same way to research, remembering a stakeholder's request or a participant's feedback hours, days, or weeks later can show active listening, supporting your fellow players, and creating a solution that sets the product as the star.

Count to 100

In Count to 100, often performed as a warm-up exercise, a group of individuals stands in a circle and attempts to count from 1 to 100 (Figure 10-8). Though this sounds simple, there are four main rules that make it more challenging:

- All players must look down at the floor, not at each other.
- A single player may not simply count all the numbers.
- You cannot go in a clear order (clockwise or counterclockwise).
- If two people speak at the same time, you start over back at 1.

This game brings together all the challenges of active listening, supporting players, and being willing to fail. Often teams find a groove and individual players start to "own" different numbers, supporting memory and building team trust in the process.

FIGURE 10-8
Design workshop warming up by counting to 100

Practical Uses of Improv

We have only scratched the surface of the fundamentals of improv. And as with any skill or muscle, it takes practice and time to understand all the nuances. Next we will explore the application of improv across product design and research.

IMPROV IN DESIGN

While this is a book on research methods, we want to address the application of improv in other areas of product design. There is no right or wrong way to use improv, and having a broader definition of its application is always helpful.

Sales

Sales meetings are essentially one large improv performance, and the research is to understand the client needs. We often craft our capability decks and sales pitches based on a request for proposal (RFP) or understanding of a client's business. The questions that are asked during these meetings are unique from pitch to pitch. As a result, we have to adjust our canned responses based on the specific needs of our prospective clients.

Voice from the Streets

Adam Polansky,
UX Strategist at Bottle Rocket Studios

In a few words, describe your job.

Bottle Rocket is a leading mobile consulting, design, and development agency. I work with major brands to define and conceptualize applications across multiple platforms that support a mobile lifestyle.

How do you use improv methods in research?

Improvisation plays an important role when you're bringing ideas to life. In my work, it begins with discovery. If you can get clients to come at things from a different perspective, you have an opportunity for broader discussion that drives bigger ideas. One example is getting everyone to pick an adjective to define project success. This gets them thinking about the essence of the goal rather than the carefully crafted objective statement they prepared. It's hard for some to let go, but it helps define where opportunities really live. It's good for stakeholders who say things like "We need an app because we need to be in the mobile channel" or "We need an app because our competitors have one."

I tell my clients that for at least a day or two, the laws of physics don't count. Right now, imagine the best possible outcomes for the user of our app, no matter how fantastic or difficult. We go into uncharted territory. I need them to imagine a great experience—one that meets a clearly stated or unmet need. If they can do that, it shifts the urgency of the conversation from "what" to "why." Solutions may not be obvious or they may seem out of reach, but if the "why" is important enough to achieve, you'd be amazed at what a dedicated team can do. I want to get clients to break away from the examples they may cling to, the "me too" mentality, and consider ways to exceed their original vision and expectations.

Physics will come crashing in soon enough, but by getting my clients off their preexisting mental script, they are more willing to explore new options that may fundamentally change the way people experience something. The truth is, it doesn't always work. You'll have varying degrees of input and buy-in because every client and project is different, but it works well enough, often enough, that it makes going to work much more enjoyable because you're making things that matter.

Don't settle for mediocrity by only doing what's expected. It's hard, but it's more fun to blaze a new trail, blow up those expectations, and do something remarkable. This is greatness!

Presentations

Whether you're delivering a sales pitch, presenting research findings, or sharing design directions, all presentations require improvisational skills. While we may write out our talking points, questions and distractions can come at any time. When you're presenting research findings, what happens if a stakeholder feels the findings are counter to their hypothesis? How do you respond? Similarly, if a design direction differs from a client's expectations, how can you shift the tone from accusatory or upset to one that exposes deeper goals, needs, and opportunities?

Idea generation

Idea generation is the closest to traditional improv during the design phase. The support we offer our teammates in a whiteboarding session requires an awareness of one another's strengths and abilities often rivaled only by a professional improv troupe. More engaging ideation activities, such as playtesting or bodystorming, are research through creative trial and error, and they rely on a number of improv skills and techniques, such as affirming, supporting our players, and reincorporation.

Workshops

Design workshops are another avenue where you can apply improv techniques. While very similar to idea generation sessions, design workshops often include stakeholders and participants outside of the core product team. This involvement with outside voices mirrors our work as researchers. Workshops may be categorized into two main groups: convergent and divergent.

Convergent workshops aim to seek consensus on a design idea. This may be the introduction of three design opportunities with the goal of integrating the best pieces from each into a single design. While you may have preferences or a hypothesis on what the direction will be, the ultimate result is unknown until it's defined.

Divergent workshops, on the other hand, seek to explore as many different avenues as possible. Participatory design sessions, paper prototyping (Figure 10-9), and card sorting are all variations on divergent design activities.

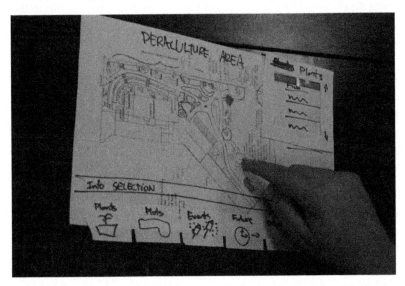

FIGURE 10-9
A paper prototype of a mobile interface

IMPROV IN RESEARCH

While improv in design is invaluable, ultimately our focus is research techniques and skills. Improv applies to research just as much as design activities. This book has outlined how different challenges may arise and how preparations and planning can help avoid them. Next are some recommendations on handling these situations when they arise despite our best efforts.

Buggy technology

We've discussed the importance of testing a prototype, having backups, and understanding the ability of different systems. When these variables inevitably happen to us, we have a choice to pack up for the day or to accept the "failure is OK" rule and press forward. Improv techniques can give us the mindset to change from a validation session to a design session, or a requirements meeting to a discussion of business needs and market segmentation.

Dud participants

Chapter 7 looked at the challenges of recruiting participants and noted that some sessions may appear less valuable than others. As we mentioned there, all participants have some value to add. If you are meeting with someone who seems out of the typical user type, see this as an opportunity to test your hypothesis with an edge case, or to explore a new hypothesis and uncover new design opportunities.

Discussion guide challenges

Discussion guides are intended as a tool to inform the conversation, not to be used as scripture. But what happens when an impromptu research session happens and no discussion guide is available? Or how do you respond when a well-crafted discussion guide turns out to be useless because a stakeholder has their own agenda during a meeting?

Embracing the flexibility of improv is key in both these situations. For impromptu research sessions, don't be afraid to lean on your teammates and share the burden of moderating. When a business stakeholder derails your well-crafted agenda, embrace it as an opportunity to set them as the star, and to listen to what they and their fellow players are saying, to better inform your research initiatives moving forward.

Exercise: Simplifying Through Improv

So far we have introduced the fundamentals of improv and a number of games for getting you into the improv mindset. The following exercise explores improv as it relates specifically to research.

1. **Write down three questions.**

   Write down three questions you have about a project you are currently working on.

2. **Talk to the mirror.**

   While standing in front of the mirror, ask yourself each question you came up with. Next, try to ask each question again just slightly differently, emphasizing different aspects of the question or using different phrasing. Repeat this as necessary until the question comes across naturally and doesn't contain flowery language, business-speak, or white noise.

Parting Thoughts

Performing and acting is often seen as something only for professional performers or skilled amateurs—you have to be a movie star, a comedian, or a Broadway performer to be able to communicate in front of an audience. In truth, though, we all do it every day at work with colleagues, at home with family, and during our commute with cab drivers or fellow subway riders.

Improvisation—thinking on your feet—is one piece of research, and one of the softer skills. While this chapter has introduced a number of games and techniques for thinking about improv in research, nothing is better than doing the real thing. Many cities host informal improv troupes and classes where you can get firsthand exposure to many of the techniques discussed here. In the meantime, our next chapter will focus on another soft skill of research: facilitation.

[11]

Facilitating Research

In a high-IQ job pool, soft skills like discipline, drive, and empathy mark those who emerge as outstanding.
—DANIEL GOLEMAN

The most unpredictable part of research, especially qualitative research, is people. Carrying on a conversation with a complete stranger while actively listening doesn't come easy. The skills needed to perform this are known as *facilitation*. Despite many books sharing techniques, the best way to learn facilitation skills is through trial and error. The goal of this chapter is to equip you with the basics to ease your learning in the field.

Soft Skills Are Hard

Some of the most important skills needed to be a successful researcher aren't taught in the classroom. These are soft skills, since they relate to social and interpersonal aspects instead of workflow or tasks. While degree programs and vocational institutions are great at teaching students how to program computers, engineer machines, and recode genetic material, they often fail at teaching the skills needed to hold a conversation or connect with another human being—whether that means introducing yourself at networking events or giving formal presentations to a group.

These skills aren't taught because, to be frank, they are hard to teach and even harder to learn. There's a lot of trial and error involved in picking up soft skills, and an ongoing feeling of failure doesn't interest a lot of students.

WHAT ARE SOFT SKILLS?

Before we get deeper into the skills needed to become a good facilitator, let's frame the term *soft skills*. It's common to relate a person's proficiency with soft skills to their EQ, or emotional quotient. EQ has emerged as a tool to describe how one uses their soft skills.[1] The higher your EQ, the more natural it is for you to pick up the skills needed to facilitate qualitative research. Similarly, with a higher EQ you'll find it easier to connect with stakeholders when providing guidance and recommendations based on your quantitative research results.

Common skills that facilitators pick up include social graces, communicating effectively, managing and leading people, noticing different personality traits, and responding to these traits. When you consider the mental and emotional juggling it takes to get these skills right, it's apparent why they aren't taught before students enter the professional world. Still, these skills not only make great researchers, but help individuals grow in their careers.

WHY SOFT SKILLS MATTER

Why are soft skills important to becoming a researcher? One of the major points of doing any form of research, qualitative or quantitative, is to create an empathetic link with your users. As you hone your EQ levels, you can better connect with users. You can learn about their successes, failures, joys, and pains. The act of facilitating requires this connection so participants feel that you are listening to their stories and genuinely care about them.

SOFT SKILLS CAN BE LEARNED

At this point you might be thinking, "Whoa! If a class can't do it, how can a book teach me soft skills so I can successfully start doing research?" Fear not! We ourselves are proof that these skills can be learned. We were once more comfortable on the sidelines, while those more experienced led research activities and client interactions. Eventually, we were put in the driver's seat and figured it out.

The biggest barrier to learning soft skills is the ability to practice them. As the old adage goes, "practice makes perfect."

---

1 Claudia S. P. Fernandez, "Emotional Intelligence in the Workplace," *Journal of Public Health Management and Practice* 13, no. 1 (2007): 80–82.

MASTERY THROUGH PRACTICE

While there are many factors to learning and mastering soft skills, the best teacher is practice. You can practice with friends and family through mock interviews. You can learn on the job by working under a lead researcher and inviting critique on your facilitation skills.

The rest of the chapter focuses on two core aspects of facilitation that enable learning: body language and microexpressions.

Body Language

Humans are expressive creatures. When having a conversation, we say way more with our body and facial expressions than we do with our words. Our physical reactions to what's being said to us, and how we use our body to emphasize what we are saying, makes talking with people entertaining. By becoming aware of both our own body language and that of others, you gain insight into the other soft skills mentioned earlier in the chapter.

WHAT IS BODY LANGUAGE?

Body language includes the different signals and cues our body gives off, some voluntary but many involuntary. These signals are paired with what we are trying to communicate. A classic example is someone throwing their arms up and waving them around when excited. You could be standing 50 feet away, and just by observing their body you know they are excited about something.

Body language is tricky because it's a mix of different signals that can mean different things depending on context, culture, and how the signals match up. As you master the art of reading body language, you'll learn to pick out different patterns and, based on the context, figure out what the most likely message is. However, even the best body language experts get it wrong sometimes and, rest assured, you will too.

WHY BODY LANGUAGE MATTERS

When you're facilitating qualitative research, the feedback you collect includes verbal responses, physical reactions to the questions asked, and physical behavior toward the product itself. These reactions are moments you want, because they're the perfect opportunity to learn more. If you see someone make a face like they've smelled spoiled milk (Figure 11-1) or they physically back away from your product, something has occurred that their subconscious has interpreted as offensive. This is your chance to ask what they are thinking and why they are reacting so negatively.

FIGURE 11-1
A disgusted expression

Without picking up on a participant's body language, you might miss a piece of evidence on why something is wrong with your product and how you could make it better.

HOW TO USE BODY LANGUAGE

As you progress in reading body language, you'll want to use it more proactively than rote observation. This shift from reactive to proactive facilitation separates junior and senior researchers.

Participants' body language

Regardless of our emotional state, our brains react to our environment with one common element: they are constantly filtering data received through our five senses. Whether we're searching for pleasure or safety, the data collected in our brain causes involuntary reactions.

When facilitating research, you need to look for these reactions to further understand people's real feelings. Body language is often more honest than what participants tell you. Participants are known to express experiences more positively than they actually perceived them so that they don't feel like a failure or feel uncomfortable giving you a negative critique to your face.

Your body language

Most researchers agree it is difficult to stay focused during every session, especially when scheduling many days of work. Being aware of your own body language is just as important as interpreting that of your participants. In this way, you prevent your fatigue from influencing participants.

To mitigate this, be aware of how you present yourself and ensure you're perceived as open and receptive. Common tricks include constant note taking, leaning in during interesting moments, and keeping your arms and shoulders open so you appear welcoming.

Mirroring

Occasionally, you get a difficult participant. Not a dud, as discussed in Chapter 7, but rather someone who holds back information and doesn't seem to trust you enough to open up. One technique to overcome this is mirroring. Mirroring is when one person's body language is imitated or reflected by the other person (Figure 11-2). Strangely, this is very natural among people. Next time you're talking with someone over coffee, pause and look at how you are both holding yourselves. You might be surprised to find aspects of your body language resemble that of the other person.

Mirroring can be used proactively to a certain extent, since it's a natural reaction. When facilitating a session with a difficult participant, purposely mirror their body language. As the session progresses, shift to more open body language and see if the participant does the same. Physical stances can directly impact our mental state, and if you get the participant to mirror your open physical positions, they are more likely to be more open with their feedback.

FIGURE 11-2

Two people mirroring each other's body language ("In Perfect Congruence" by Gideon is licensed under CC BY 2.0)

KEY BODY SIGNALS

The following are several classic signals that hint at another person's mental state (see Figure 11-3). We want to caution you against fixating on a single signal and drawing conclusions from it, however. It's important to take into account all signals observed in the context of the conversation.

Open arms and legs

Oftentimes, when your body is in an open position, your mindset is also open. This can mean when you are presented with ideas, you might be more approachable and agreeable overall.

Closed arms and legs

The opposite is true if your body is in a closed position. It's likely that your mindset is defensive and potentially closed off.

Spread-out arms and legs

Everyone has their own personal bubble, and sometimes stretching out your arms and taking a wide stance reflects an attempt to expand your personal space or assert your overall presence.

Leg positioning

Your legs like to point in the direction you want to move. For example, if your legs are crossed and pointed at the door, there's a chance that you may not want to be wherever you are.

Head movements

When you look up it can indicate that you're accessing your imagination and potentially being deceitful. When you look down it can indicate that you're accessing your memory and potentially being more truthful.

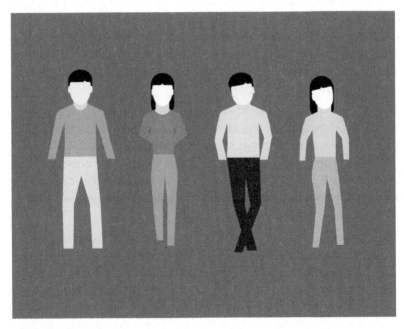

FIGURE 11-3
A variety of common body postures: open arms, closed arms, closed legs, and open legs (left to right)

Voice from the Streets

Kyle Soucy, Usable Interface

In a few words, describe your job.

I am an independent UX consultant that specializes in conducting user research and usability testing.

How do body language and soft skills impact the type of research you conduct?

One of my favorite research methods is *collaging*. Collaging is a projective technique by which participants select images that represent how they feel about a particular topic (e.g., "Select pictures that reflect your experience with using *x*"). The participants then explain to the moderator the reason they chose each image. Collaging is typically done during the *early* stages of product development, when user requirements are being gathered. The method is also helpful at any time in the product's development if you feel the design team is having trouble understanding and identifying with the users. Sometimes designers need to step back and remember exactly whom they are designing for.

The reason why I love collaging so much is because it always results in the participant sharing something personal or taboo that would otherwise be hard to discuss with a complete stranger. An image can be a powerful stimulus that evokes a strong response, triggers a memory, and draws out feelings that exist below a person's own level of awareness. I've had several conversations with participants about their collages that have led to them shedding tears.

Since this method is so highly effective at getting participants to open up, I have to be extra vigilant to pick up on any cues that they may not want to continue discussing the topic. I often use the analogy of entering a room where you don't want to be; participants may not necessarily want to walk through that door that they've unlocked so easily with their collage. In order to make sure the participant is comfortable I pay close attention to their body language, especially their facial expressions. The moment I sense that they're feeling unease, I ask how they are doing and remind them that we can stop at any time—which is why it's also equally important for me to keep my own body language in check. When a participant shares something with me that may be rather shocking, it's imperative that I try to conceal any level of judgment, disgust, surprise, etc., from them. I'm mindful not to raise my eyebrows, scrunch my brow, wrinkle my nose in abhorrence, or do anything else that may reveal my true response. As a UX researcher, it's imperative to remain neutral and unbiased. Sometimes it can be challenging to stay in character, and being prepared for it is key.

Microexpressions

Your body isn't the only thing communicating signals; facial expressions also add to nonverbal communication. Microexpressions are the subtle ways your face reacts, sometimes voluntary and other times not. One example is the natural crow's feet that appear around your eyes when you smile (see Figure 11-4). If it is a genuine smile, those muscles around the eye contract involuntarily.

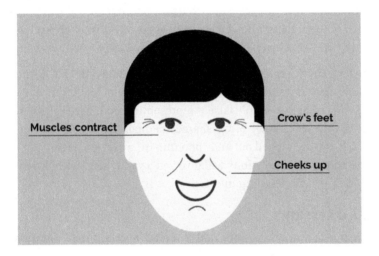

FIGURE 11-4
A genuine smile contains many microexpressions, including raised cheeks and contracted muscles that cause crow's feet around a person's eyes

There are many different kinds of microexpressions, and entire courses of study about this mode of communication. Knowing they exist and how to use them in the context of research gives you another advantage when you're conducting research in person.[2]

---

2 To learn more about the importance of microexpressions, listen to "Microexpressions: More Than Meets The Eye," a 2013 NPR interview with law enforcement officer David Matsumoto (*http://www.npr.org/2013/05/10/182861380/microexpressions-more-than-meets-the-eye*).

WHY MICROEXPRESSIONS MATTER

Not everyone acts naturally during research sessions. That's because research is unnatural in the first place, and people might feel obligated to tell or show you what they think you want to hear. By watching a participant's microexpressions and body language, you can redirect or follow up with probing questions to better understand how they really use or feel about your product.

HOW TO USE MICROEXPRESSIONS

The best way to use microexpressions is to couple observation skills with active listening skills. When trying to understand how someone uses your product, pay attention to both their words and their physical reactions. You will see hints of truth, deceit, and reservation that inform your probing and follow-up questions. Actively observing in this way means you are less likely to miss anything worth capturing.

Your own microexpressions play a part too, because the participant's subconscious is watching you. After a number of sessions, you will need to ensure you aren't falsely representing your level of interest. This is why, in Chapter 6, we shared methods for managing energy levels. If you are tapped out and "phoning in" a session, your body language and microexpressions will give you away, regardless of how well you think you are feigning interest.

KEY EXPRESSIONS

There are a number of common microexpressions that you should actively look for, as cross-cultural studies have shown that, although the interpretation of expressions is universal, the expression of emotions through the face changes depending on social context.[3] The expressions on this list are generic enough that just about everyone does them and, if you pay attention, you will be able to better predict when you should probe deeper or just move on to the next line of questioning (see Figure 11-5).

---

3 Vinay Bettadapura, "Face Expression Recognition and Analysis: The State of the Art," *arXiv* (March 2012).

Surprise

Eyes open wide and jaw dropped. Something has happened that the participant didn't expect and you should try to learn what it was, why it surprised them, and what they were expecting.

Fear

Eyes wide, mouth barely open, and forehead winkled. The participant might feel like they made a mistake and have failed in some way. You will want to know why they are feeling this way and how to ease this feeling.

Disgust

Teeth bared, nose wrinkled, and eyes slightly closed. Whatever the participant was saying or doing does not agree with them and they feel "offended." Get to the heart of this offense and try to learn why they feel this way.

Anger

Hard stare, closed and tense lips, and nostrils possibly open wide. Something has made the participant go on the defensive. Try to understand what is causing this reaction and why it happened.

Happiness

Broad smile, crow's feet around the eyes, and raised cheeks. The product or topic on hand clearly is one that makes the participant feel good. Probe into why they feel so happy about what's happening and try to probe the triggers of this response.

Sadness

Pouting lips and drawn-in eyes. An action or conversation has triggered the participant to feel bad. You will want to understand what the trigger was and how it might have been avoided.

Contempt

Partial fake smile and squinting eyes. The participant doesn't trust what just happened or whatever you have just said. Probe into where this distrust is coming from and how it's affecting the participant.

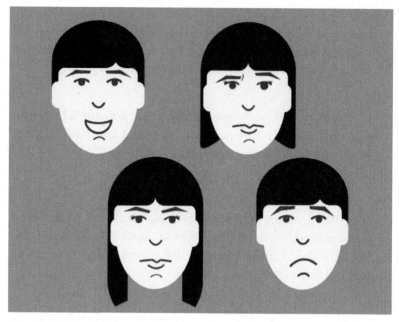

FIGURE 11-5

A variety of common facial expressions: delight (top left), worry (top right), frustration (bottom left), and sadness (bottom right)

Cultural Implications

If working on a product that has a global presence, you will encounter situations where nonverbal cues from one culture don't apply to another. Something as simple as the thumbs up to show that everything is OK in one culture might be an offensive symbol that can ruin a research session in another. Fear not: there are steps you can follow to navigate these murky waters and avoid awkward situations.

DO YOUR HOMEWORK

First, research different social norms and the background of any country you'll be conducting research in. What documentation from other researchers can you use to prepare? You'll want to research topics including how authority is perceived, how gender roles differ, how foreigners are viewed, and what topics or gestures are a sign of respect or disrespect.

One of the best places to learn about local customs and social norms are tourism sites. This content has been curated for years to ensure visitors have all the information they need to enjoy their trip and avoid negative experiences with locals.

COME FROM A PLACE OF RESPECT

Research aside, approach everyone from a place of respect. If appropriate, be ready to apologize quickly and often as you stumble through a session. Because the context of your visit is to conduct research, there is a degree of forgiveness allowed by those you encounter when mistakes are made.

Exercise: Reading Nonverbal Communication

Reading nonverbal communication is hard to practice, as it typically requires other people. There are a few methods you can work through, however, to refine your skills.

MIMICRY

Actors are masters at performing with both their words and their bodies. Pick a favorite movie and mimic the actions and expressions that are happening on screen during the dramatic moments of the film. Try to learn the different combinations of movements and facial expressions that the actors use to act out the scene, as these will be the same combinations and expressions you'll observe in the real world.

OBSERVATION

Many researchers claim people watching as a favorite hobby. Put this hobby to use by watching how people react to each other in public spaces, or how they react when having a conversation. Try to pick up on the different emotions that are being expressed and see what kind of reactions they get. The best place to do this kind of practice is in public spaces, like a shopping mall, coffee shop, or an airport.

INQUIRY

If you want to get some direct critique on your new observation skills, ask a close friend for help. Start with a normal conversation. Look for certain nonverbal cues and ask your friend what they are feeling or thinking. Occasionally, guess their thoughts or feelings and ask if you're right or wrong. This can be a bit awkward, but it's one of the only times you'll get candid feedback on how well your observation skills are progressing.

Parting Thoughts

The best way to learn and grow facilitation skills is through practice. When you start practicing, you will make mistakes. Each mistake teaches you valuable lessons and hones your skills.

The biggest hurdle for one of the authors was overcoming social awkwardness. Sitting down and talking with strangers was terrifying. Over time, however, he found his groove and is now less of a nervous wreck. Running research activities, especially qualitative ones, gets easier with time. Keep at it and don't let the little mistakes that only you notice stop you. Once you have the research under your belt, the real fun begins—sharing with your team and organizing your findings!

[12]

Debrief Sessions

There are three classes of people: Those who see. Those who see when they are shown. Those who do not see.
—LEONDARDO DA VINCI

> Research is about observing tasks, questioning hypotheses, and validating concepts to define a more successful product. No research is complete without sharing observations. And sharing starts in the field with debrief sessions. While the remainder of this book looks at the organization and communication of research data, this chapter focuses specifically on communication that occurs continually during research.

What Are Debrief Sessions?

In Chapter 6, we described the pacing and cadence of schedules, including the "recharging" time between research sessions where prototypes are reset and the team grabs a cup of coffee. Debriefs, simply put, are conversations you have during those times. These debrief sessions don't need to be planned, though their purpose and goals are consistent.

PLANNED DEBRIEF SESSIONS

Planned debrief sessions may be as short as five minutes after a research session, or as formal as an end-of-day discussion with all observers and business stakeholders. In either case, the goal of the session is to quickly go around the group and identify what went well, what could be improved upon, and actionable next steps for the duration of the research initiative.

AD HOC DEBRIEF SESSIONS

Ad hoc debrief sessions can take place at any time, though we recommend waiting until after a research session is over. More impromptu debrief sessions may take place after a particularly good or bad session, or if new business requirements are identified and need to be brought to the project team's attention.

Why Debrief?

Nobody can be everywhere. And nobody can remember everything. And no single perspective is perfect or right. With project teams consisting of multiple skill sets—from design, research, development, and strategy—each observer has a different perspective with which they interpret their observations (see Figure 12-1). Each perspective carries different concerns, needs, and questions. Add to this the variety of business stakeholders, and the complexity multiplies exponentially. A familiar metaphor for this is the multiple accounts that different eyewitnesses bring to a case; their personal interpretations vary depending on their perspective, biases, and focus. Debrief sessions allow project teams to align on findings and use a common language.

FIGURE 12-1
Team in a debrief session

Voice from the Streets

Bibiana Nunes, Senior Manager eCommerce for adidas Group in Mexico

How do you debrief with your team throughout research initiatives?

When we launched Reebok.mx, I was so focused on not repeating the mistakes that happened when we launched adidas.mx that I took for granted the things that went well and lost sight of them. I was so focused on the trees that I lost sight of the forest.

Our biggest hurdle when launching Reebok.mx was the marketing campaign: it was go-live day, everything was set up, the site had been tested thoroughly, teams had traveled, product was online, and product campaigns were on...what could go wrong? The marketing campaigns were not fully active, which meant traffic was scarce despite weekly meetings for two months to make sure everything was ready.

I was expecting for everyone to do their part. By meeting with my team afterward I learned that my expectations were not communicated properly. The people collaborating with me were not aware of the responsibilities I had placed on them but didn't clearly communicate to them. I also learned that sending emails does not equal communicating expectations.

Had I not met with them, I would not have seen this. It's not about being Captain Hindsight, it's about creating a space for the people that walk with you to share their perspective of an experience. Despite being on the same project, each of our perspectives is a different one. Their perspective will open up your boundaries and your confirmation bias to realize what role you could have played that could have made the difference.

For me it was also important to be in listening mode. When receiving feedback, my team didn't want my justification on why things went the way they did. They wanted their side of the story to be heard and understood. And from my side, listening to their stories allowed me to see where I took wrong turns.

In the end, having this debriefing session helped us understand and identify where the gaps were, united us as a team, and prevented the snowball effect of placing blame on others instead of accepting responsibility on the role each of us played in the project. It's a place where we learn from each other and ourselves, allowing us to grow individually as well as a team.

VALIDATE GOALS

In Chapter 2 we discussed how research involves asking good questions. And in Chapter 6 we discussed the importance of crafting a hypothesis. One of the greatest benefits of the debrief session is getting to see in real time how those questions and hypotheses are measured.

When crafting questions, you might think you have an open dialogue, only to realize that your questions are leading or limited in scope. Debrief sessions help you step away from your own perspective and, by playing back tape or simply discussing with your team, fine-tune questions in real time. Discussion guides are exactly that—guides—and while there are sometimes concerns about changing tactics midway through research, it is better to realign questions than to gather less-than-ideal feedback.

Your hypothesis can also be tested in real time. For those with scientific backgrounds, this differs from a double blind study, where observers do not know the goals of the research and therefore cannot impact data. UX research is not clinical, and does not pretend to adhere to strict protocols. Being able to see how results unfold in real time gives you insight into how much more research is necessary. If you have 10 participants scheduled and have enough answers after 4, a debrief session could save you time and money. On the other hand, realizing after 8 participants that there are still unknown questions can give you enough lead time to schedule additional sessions.

KEEP THE HOME OFFICE INFORMED

It is rare that everyone on a project team can travel for research. You also have the constraint of having only two to three people in the same room as the participant. Thus, it is very important to keep your project team and business stakeholders informed throughout a research initiative.

Moderated research initiatives

Moderated research initiatives, especially for research involving travel, require keeping the home office informed. This provides a sense of security that research is happening and the process is moving forward. The following popular methods of communicating with the home office are listed from easiest to more complex:

Email

A simple email between sessions can keep your project team informed (see Figure 12-2). A message like "We just met with Bill, head of accounting, and got some good validation on the task flow about procurement. Something interesting came up around liability we should ask the client about later" is more than enough.

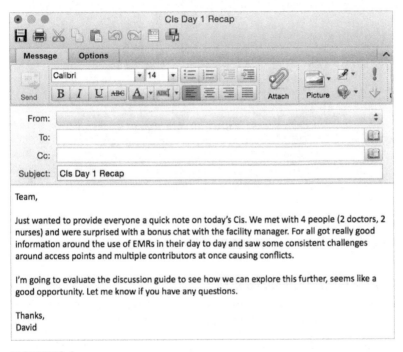

FIGURE 12-2
Sample debrief email

Phone

Email is great for brevity, but sometimes a phone call is preferred. This may be a scheduled call or a "drop-in" to a project manager or team lead. The information doesn't need to be any more detailed than the email. If you are looking to confirm timely information, such as scheduling, phone is preferred for its speed.

Video recap

For longer initiatives, it is sometimes preferred to "see" your project team, even remotely. With the advent of screen-sharing and video conference tools, you can schedule end-of-day recaps with your project teams. This is particularly helpful with teams located across multiple time zones, as it can help build rapport. Figure 12-3 illustrates a remote debrief session.

FIGURE 12-3
Remote debrief session via screen share and webcam

Remote research implications

When performing remote, unmoderated research, meeting to debrief is often easier because travel is not involved. The challenge lies in the multiple, parallel paths research can take. With remote research, you are no longer limited to two researchers for each participant; multiple participants can walk through a remote test simultaneously.

For remote research, it is important to have team members tasked with reviewing incoming content as quickly as possible. Then, by scheduling daily meetings, the team can quickly verify the information gathered is appropriate and raise any concerns or proposed changes in a timely manner.

Quantitative research implications

Debrief sessions for quantitative research are very similar to those for remote research. In quantitative research, data is being gathered passively and across many streams. Daily, or even weekly, touchpoints allow for regularly checking in on the data and sharing it with a project team. Constant communication is critical in high-volume environments, such as commerce platforms or sales tools. In these situations, A/B tests can provide feedback in a matter of hours or days (depending on the test's scale) and can validate a decision or prevent a larger problem from arising.

Keep clients informed

Ultimately we all work for a client. This may be our own organization if we work in house, or it may be a third party. Keeping the clients informed of the status of the research is just as important as keeping your project team informed. Think back to the challenges you may have faced selling research to managers and clients. Debrief sessions offer an opportunity to see the value of this work in real time and can make it easier to sell future research.

The tone of a client debrief may change slightly. Whereas with your project team you may discuss findings, observations, and updates in real time, you often want to provide a higher-level view to clients. Despite this, clients will ask what results you are observing, and there is a fine line between being too vague and too detailed while a research initiative is under way. A common way to ease client debrief sessions is by inviting clients to observe research in real time. This way, they become more active members of the research team and can act as your champion with the broader client team.

Keep the team informed

For research initiatives involving many teams working simultaneously, daily debrief sessions keep everyone in sync. It allows teams to identify challenges that are localized to a specific region because of technology constraints, cultural differences, or something else altogether. If a challenge, observation, or opportunity arises across multiple locations, it allows the team to address the hurdle in a uniform manner.

TRACK HIGHLIGHTS IN REAL TIME

For any research initiative you will collect a lot of data. For a single 60-minute contextual inquiry, it is not uncommon to leave with 75–100 individual data points, or individual pieces of information. Chapter 13 will go into more detail on the analysis and organization of this information. Multiply this across a number of participants and a pool of observers, and you can be faced with thousands of data points from a simple five-person study. With this in mind, it is critical to start tracking data early and often. Next we offer a few methods that help with this process. And while specific tools are mentioned, these are meant to be representative of the type of tools available, not prescriptive recommendations.

Spreadsheets

Spreadsheets can be so cumbersome that many designers are hesitant to use them. But when you're looking at multiple participants and observers, spreadsheets are often the gold standard of organizing separate notes. While there is no wrong way to set up a data collection spreadsheet, Figure 12-4 illustrates a sample spreadsheet.

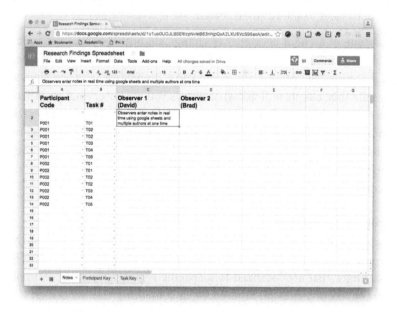

FIGURE 12-4
Sample data spreadsheet

Affinity diagrams

Switching from digital to analog, sometimes a good wall and stack of sticky notes is sufficient for real-time tracking. Taking time each day to write down key findings and observations is often enough to stay on top of research analysis later on. While one challenge with affinity diagrams is the requirement for a shared, physical space, this also acts to your benefit, because business stakeholders can drop in and engage in the process in a curated manner. Figure 12-5 illustrates a project room covered in sticky notes.

FIGURE 12-5
Affinity diagram for a large business system

Digital affinity diagrams

Technology allows you to adapt traditional affinity diagrams in more digital ways. Trello and other digital tools (Figure 12-6) enable remote sharing and collaboration.

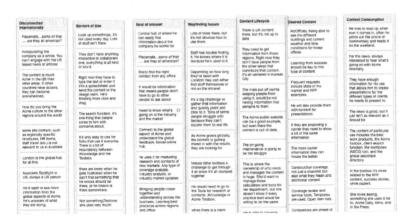

FIGURE 12-6
Digital affinity diagram tool illustrating research for a company intranet

Mural.ly is another collaborative tool that enables the creation of poster spaces for sharing inspiration (Figure 12-7). And for those familiar with the Google tools, Google Drawing is one that can be adapted for remote collaboration. Each of these tools has its pros and cons, and we encourage you to try as many as possible to see what works for you and your team.

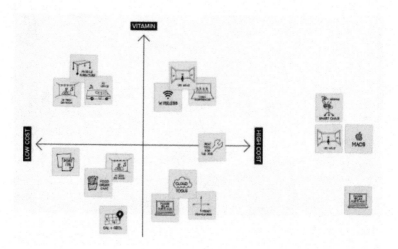

FIGURE 12-7

Illustration of Mural.ly from *https://mural.co*

Highlight reel

For the truly adventurous, a highlight reel (Figure 12-8) collects video and audio snippets from a research initiative to tell a piece of the story. This requires recording and the necessary consent forms, and is often used in larger projects to sell the research upstream to senior stake-holders. During research, it is common for observers to annotate where something interesting or exciting happens. This makes it easier to find that clip later for editing and integration into a highlight reel. Reels don't need to last longer than five minutes. Tracking the content early is key to being able to consolidate information later on.

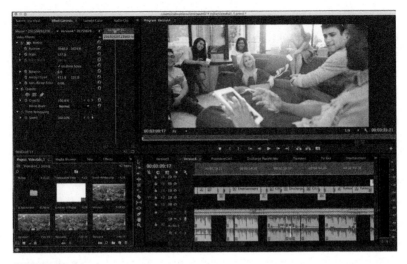

FIGURE 12-8
A highlight reel being edited

Debrief Informs Iteration

So far we have talked about the value of debrief sessions for keeping your project teams informed. Equally important are the iterations in process that come from frequent, open communication. Research, like design, is iterative, and this process of evaluating and change happens only through sharing findings and concerns with team members and stakeholders.

RESEARCH IN THE OPEN

Research is part of the collaborative design process. Collaborating in research starts by sharing your approach and findings early and often. While it can be frightening to share raw, unfiltered content with clients, providing access to this material early and often can help build relationships and accelerate synthesis later on.

For a client, access to video or an end-of-day email summarizing activities brings transparency to the process. This may highlight new opportunities for future validation and expose gaps in your or the client's understanding of the approach. Some practitioners shy away from sharing raw data because information out of context might create more questions than it answers. While that outcome is possible, framing the information with the goals can mitigate the risk.

For your project team, communicating your research allows checks and balances. Whether you are performing multiple parallel paths of research or simply communicating to other team members, open communication allows an escalation of concerns early and often, mitigating risk.

MITIGATE RISK

Nobody wants to go through a weeks-long research initiative only to find out something went wrong. Debrief sessions allow for iterating on technology and process to avoid larger issues down the line.

This issue may be something as minor as the microphone not recording audio or a poor phone connection. It may also be something more significant like the wrong order of questions or a persistent bug in a prototype. By having these conversations early and often, you can adjust the protocol on the fly and have more actionable results later on. We recommend you keep track of when and what changes are made to a research protocol, as any sudden spikes or changes in data should be related back to changes in how research was performed.

Exercise: Discussing Observations

The information that gets discussed during debrief sessions is best sourced from the team that was involved in observing the research. Getting comfortable with sending out debrief notes involves gathering everyone together to discuss what each person saw. The following exercise describes how to facilitate this meeting.

1. **Gather the team.**

   Gather your team to discuss the observations from research, stakeholder meetings, or team meetings that recently occurred.

2. **Write down observations.**

   Each team member should write down three to five observations that stood out during the sessions being reviewed. This should be done in silence to avoid influencing one another.

3. **Gather and discuss.**

Organize the observations using a whiteboard or online collaboration space. Go around and have each person explain what made them write down their observations. With one person as the note taker, ask for additional feedback for each observation to see if others noticed anything that stood out.

4. **Share.**

Save the notes to a shared network. Sharing within your organization and other teams on related projects is suggested, though in practice is often difficult.

Parting Thoughts

Debrief sessions are not difficult, but they do require a degree of intent and planning. When thinking of a debrief session, don't try to make it a formal presentation or review. Instead, think of it as a "How was your day?" discussion. In this way, you have a conversation with your team and stakeholders. Everyone will feel more engaged and more motivated to contribute to the project as a whole.

With this in mind, we will now move into Part IV, where we will explore the nuances of how to communicate your research findings to teams and stakeholders alike.

Part IV

Analysis and Reporting

RESEARCH INFORMS THE EVOLUTION of a product's development and must be analyzed and reported to stakeholders. This final part of the book will provide you with the fundamentals to take your hard-earned findings and use them to progress your product to the next level.

Making Sense of the Mess
Anyone who has planned a large event, written a research paper, coordinated people, or organized information knows the importance of an organization schema. Chapter 13 introduces research analysis by first defining data points, exploring their use, and progressing to different approaches of analysis.

Communicating Insights
While the first step to acting on research findings is analysis, you ultimately need to communicate these findings to stakeholders and teammates alike. Just as many research methods leverage techniques from other fields, communicating insights can leverage lessons from storytelling. In Chapter 14 we will explore the basics of a narrative arc and some common tools and techniques for reporting research findings.

Getting the Most Out of Research
While research is a critical part of any product lifecycle, it is important to bring your findings and activities to all phases of a project. In this way, the impact of research is not limited to a single phase. Chapter 15 concludes this part and the book with examples of and resources for how to spread research's impact beyond the immediate scope of an individual research session, synthesis diagram, or presentation of findings.

[13]

Making Sense of the Mess

It takes as much energy to wish as it does to plan.
—ELEANOR ROOSEVELT

If you've made it this far, you've successfully asked questions pertinent to your work, screened and recruited participants, and conducted qualitative or quantitative research. There is no rest for the weary researcher, though, and the most integral part of any protocol is just ahead: research analysis, or making sense of the mess, as Abby Covert, author of *How to Make Sense of Any Mess*, calls it. This chapter will demystify many of the challenges and hurdles pertaining to analysis.

Why Bother with Analysis?

Project teams often want to go from research directly to design and production. The assumption is that because researchers heard the data, they can communicate the key needs verbally or in an email, and the team can save time and money by moving ahead with the project. This overlooks the opportunities analysis offers and creates more challenges than it solves.

By having a formal analysis process, your project team and stakeholders are able to create a shared understanding of what was heard and how your project goals might shift. This also empowers the team to communicate through a common language. Before getting much further in how to analyze research in UX and product design, however, we will highlight how research analysis is performed in fields outside of our own.

MANUFACTURING AND ENGINEERING

This book started with a history of research in Chapter 1 and noted some manufacturing and industrial applications. What we didn't mention is how to perform research analysis. In automobile design, research is used both for manufacturing efficiencies and safety improvements. Think back to the last car commercial you saw. There is a good chance it featured a crash test dummy (Figure 13-1). While the tests shown in the commercial are staged, they are not for marketing purposes only. Analyzing data from tests informs the design of crumple zones, airbag placement, and emergency detection systems and thus increases our overall safety on the road.

FIGURE 13-1
Crash test dummy in a car commercial

Beyond automobile design, architects and engineers use computers and 3-D models to test the stability of their designs (Figure 13-2). Without structural analysis, the bridge we drive over in our statistically safe car might not handle the weight of rush hour!

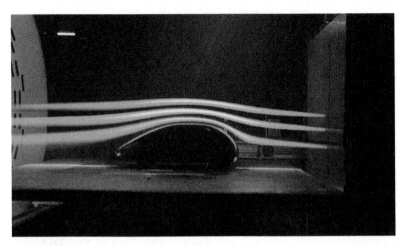

FIGURE 13-2
3-D model representing a wind tunnel

GAME DESIGN

Stepping closer to our work as product designers, we can look at game design as another avenue for testing and analysis. Often called *play-testing*, this form of research analysis involves playing out games in real life. For board and card games, this can be as literal as writing out rules on index cards and seeing where the hurdles in gameplay are. For games that will eventually be played out on the screen, this may involve a degree of role-playing (pun intended) and activities similar to bodystorming, mentioned in Chapter 10. In either case, research and testing help the game designers understand where a game could be improved, and data analysis highlights these opportunities.

Analysis in Product Design

In product design, research analysis is based on data captured on the screen or research notes written down. In either case, we don't get to crash cars, build 3-D models, or play card games. So how do we analyze data in design when we don't get all these fancy tools? It starts with a data point.

WHAT IS A DATA POINT?

A data point can be defined as a single thought, concept, or idea. This applies to all forms of research, both qualitative and quantitative. Still, the nuances of what makes a data point vary depending on your method and approach.

Quantitative data points

For quantitative research, such as analytics or surveys, a data point is a single cell in your spreadsheet (Figure 13-3). This may be the time a user spent on a page, the number of times a button was clicked, or whether a user scrolled or not. The key is to keep data points as discrete as possible so that they may be organized, sorted, and visualized in the most effective way possible. It is not uncommon for a survey that spans hundreds of participants or a series of analytics to result in thousands of data points. Fortunately, quantitative data is already digitized and can be analyzed en masse quite efficiently.

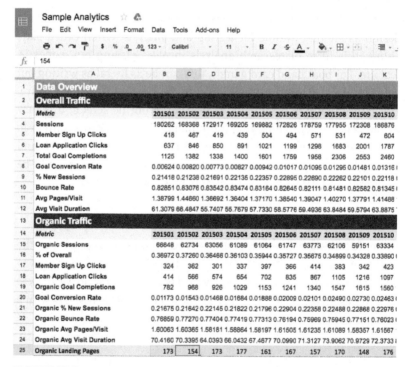

FIGURE 13-3

Analytics spreadsheet showing sample data from a quantitative study (courtesy of Andy Scott)

Qualitative data points

With qualitative research, the idea of a data point is a little less cut-and-dried. Rather than measuring a 1–10 satisfaction ranking, you have a conversation to filter through. It is often tempting for newer researchers to try to combine many data points into a single note or item.

Just as with quantitative data points, though, it is important to consider how the data might be used later on and to keep data points distinct. For instance, the data point "Participant found checkout flow complex and wished that guest checkout was available like their competitors" is two separate data points: "Participant found checkout flow complex" and "Participant desires guest checkout flow." With this distinction, it is not uncommon for teams to collect over 100 data points per interview over six 60-minute interviews.

USING DATA POINTS

With hundreds or even thousands of data points floating around, how is anybody supposed to start organizing the information, let alone enact positive change? We will start by outlining a process for coding, or cataloging, the data and discuss theory around organizing the information. We will then share some common methods for analysis.

How to code

While there is no one way to code data points, there are a few common practices. The first step is to create a master list of your participants and assign each a number. Don't get too creative here—P1, P2, P3, and so on works well for simplicity and for anonymity (Figure 13-4).

Once you have your master sheet, start to enter data in your spreadsheet. While affinity diagrams and other physical tools (covered later in this chapter) are great for collaboration, a central, digital document provides redundancy when the air conditioner kicks on mid-weekend, blowing sticky notes halfway down the hall. When entering data, reserve a column for the participant code and, if you can, the task that the data point refers to. In the next column, write your data point, one per cell. At this stage, your goal is to capture the data from research in a central location. For quantitative research this may be as simple as cleaning up some existing data and creating pivot tables, while for qualitative research this process may take significant effort.

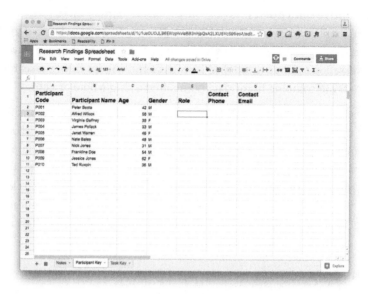

FIGURE 13-4
Sample participant master sheet

Only after the data has all been coded can you start to analyze at a broader level. To do this, you need to understand how to handle repetitive data points and data points that may apply to multiple themes.

Dealing with repeats

When dealing with hundreds of data points, you will come across the same piece of information multiple times. This is a good thing. When participants repeat information, it's a sign of a trend. Write down each data point, even if it feels redundant. When you start to visualize the data, tools like Tomer Sharon's Rainbow Spreadsheets (*https://www.smashingmagazine.com/2013/04/rainbow-spreadsheet-collaborative-ux-research-tool*) can help show data trends at a glance (Figure 13-5). In this tool, feedback is displayed in rows, and participant codes in columns. Color-coding each participant and highlighting cells where they have a data point makes trends more apparent.

Assigning multiple homes

It is also common for data points to fit in multiple groups throughout analysis. For instance, if a participant said, "The system times me out too quickly," this might be grouped under a section on security as well as one on session time. If it seems important to list a piece of information twice, then do just that. Whether with a digital tool or analog process, record the note twice and then mark it with a symbol, usually "x2," to flag it as a duplicate.

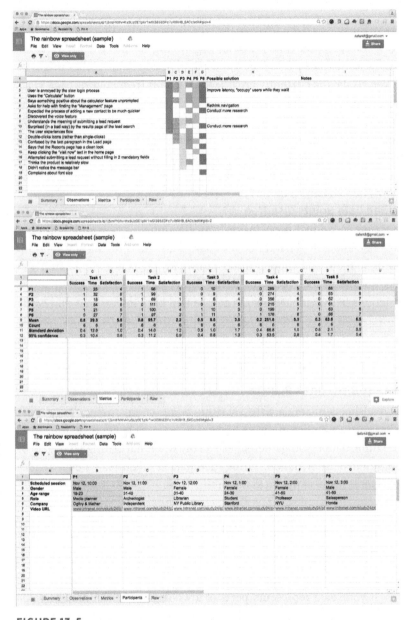

FIGURE 13-5

Tomer Sharon's Rainbow Spreadsheet

Different points of view

The reason you talk to a variety of participants is because each person has a unique perspective. It is your task to take these different opinions and identify common threads and opportunities. One approach to balancing these individual biases is to look at data from many perspectives.

As you organize data, invite team members into the process to see how they interpret the content. After organizing in one particular order, take a picture or save a version and ask what other approaches might be taken. If data is currently organized based on frequency of page visits or time on task, what insights might be revealed if you look instead at user demographics? How might organizing data points by page differ from organizing them by task or function? Each of these perspectives tells a different story, and only by identifying as many as possible can you determine what is most important.

When data points disagree

Because individual participants vary, data points may directly contradict one another. What if one user says a feature is the most important thing to them and another finds it unwieldy? This is an opportunity to ask questions such as: What is the source of the feedback? What distinctions between participants can be tied back to personas and workflows? Or is there something larger impacting your data collection? By answering these questions and looking at the data from various points of view, you'll get richer interpretations.

MEASURING DATA POINTS

Spreadsheets full of data are a starting point for organizing data points. There are a number of pivots and charts you can generate to represent the information you gathered, especially when navigating large sets of quantitative information. While each data set requires its own visualization, some best practices are outlined here:

Use a valuable scale
> If your data is on a 1–5 scale, don't display the chart on a 1–100 scale.

Use valuable visualizations
> If your data represents parts of a whole, a pie chart may be valuable. But don't use a pie chart if you are showing growth over time or content that doesn't compare well.

Use embellishments sparingly

This is a frustration we have with PowerPoint. It is all too easy to add drop shadows, gradients, and reflections to charts. These embellishments, while adding a sense of flare, at best distract from the data and at worst confuse it. Figure 13-6 showcases some good and bad samples.

Clean Visualizations

- **Simple bulleted list with branded colors**
  - Sub bullet
- **Additional Note**

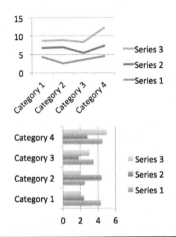

Overly Embellished Visualizations

- ⌘ **Over embellished list with branded colors**
  - ⌘ Sub bullet
- ⌘ **Additional Note**

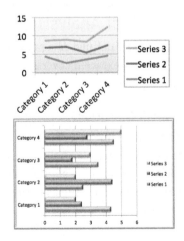

FIGURE 13-6
Samples of good and bad PowerPoints

SETTING ASIDE TIME

The process of coding and cataloging data is time-consuming. While there is no recipe for success, we recommend a minimum of three hours of analysis and collating for every hour of research. For instance, if you conducted 10 one-hour contextual inquiries, plan for a minimum of 30 hours of analysis. This number is a little harder for quantitative research, but it is still common to plan higher than lower.

Using the 30-hour example, the process may be generally divided as follows:

- 8–12 hours reviewing recordings and coding notes
- 8–12 hours organizing and reorganizing data
- 8–12 hours analyzing data

When reviewing recordings and notes, you are in the first stage of coding data. During this time you want to create your individual data points. This often takes slightly longer than the actual sessions, as you might be listening, pausing, and rewinding tapes to capture data correctly. The organizing and reorganizing phase is when you'll group the different perspectives, duplicates, and contradicting data in various ways. Lastly, analyzing data is the process of identifying the opportunities. This takes a good amount of time, as the broader team is invited for review and collaboration. The rest of this chapter will look at common tools for analysis.

Methods of Analysis

So far we have defined data points and how to go about organizing them differently. Next we'll cover some of the most common approaches to analyzing that data.

AFFINITY DIAGRAMS

Affinity diagramming (Figure 13-7) is the process of organizing data into logical groups at a holistic level. While there are many digital tools to affinity diagram, we suggest you first try with stacks of colored sticky notes. Use the following as a primer:

1. Write each individual data point on a sticky note. Use only one color, usually the default yellow, for this step. If your data points are digitized in an Excel spreadsheet, you can actually purchase printer sheets that make creating the initial stack of notes a breeze. Don't forget to include the participant code on each sticky.

2. On a large, clean whiteboard (sticky notes adhere better to whiteboards and glass than paint), take turns reading each data point out loud and stick it to the wall. As you encounter data points that relate to other data points, group them together.

3. As clusters start to have 10–15 data points each, give them a group title and list that with another colored sticky note. If you find two groups are related, use a third color for a section label.

4. Don't be afraid of reorganizing the content as you move along. Sticky notes are cheap.

5. At the end of the process, take a picture and digitize the diagram in an Excel sheet or other visualization for reflection later on.

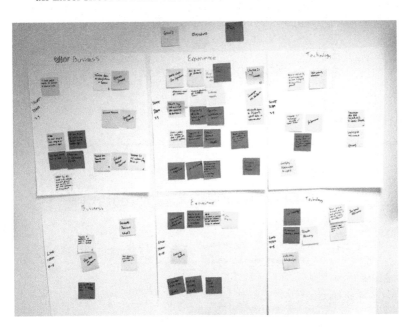

FIGURE 13-7
Affinity diagram

QUADRANT MAPPING

Where affinity diagramming takes data points and groups them in an open manner, quadrant mapping maps data to an established grid. One common approach is called *SWOT analysis*. SWOT stands for strengths, weaknesses, opportunities, and threats. Draw this 2×2 grid on the wall, and with the same sticky notes as before, read each one aloud and determine which of the four quadrants it fits into (Figure 13-8). For instance, improving the guest checkout flow is an opportunity for any commerce platform, whereas an on-demand offering may be a threat to a brick-and-mortar store. Approaches like this are particularly helpful when you're meeting with business leaders to impact strategic roadmaps.

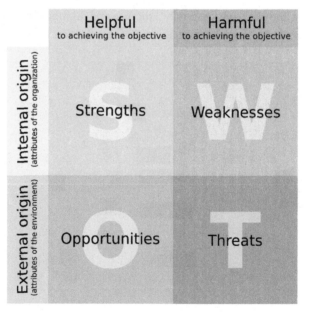

FIGURE 13-8
SWOT analysis chart

For more information on quadrant mapping techniques, see *Gamestorming* by Sunni Brown, James Macanufo, and Dave Gray (O'Reilly).

Voice from the Streets

Abby Covert

In a few words, describe your job.

As an information architect, it is my job to help organizations make sense of messes of language and structure.

How do you approach research analysis?

When I start a new project to improve the language and structure of a product, the organization I am working within doesn't always have a clear understanding of what is actually wrong with what they have. Instead, they have a hunch (or data) that isn't serving them as well as they wish it were.

The first step I take is to reverse-engineer diagrams of the current language and structure so it can be "seen" and discussed. This is like an architect drawing a blueprint of an existing space in order to discuss a remodel.

One of the most important diagrams that I often make is an association map of language. By interviewing stakeholders and users I get the conversational language used to describe the product. Then I start to "mine" for language used within things like the organization's websites, marketing materials, help documentation, customer service scripts, and database schemas. By making an association map of all of these sources, I can show how inconsistencies of language are getting in the way of clarity.

Recently, I was working with a startup that had acquired two other startups. By creating a language association map, I was able to show that the organization had up to 14 labels for the same or similar concepts. This was keeping them from being clear with their customers, made onboarding of new employees more difficult, and created technical debt that was slowing down projects all over the organization. At the time I made this map, the startup was preparing to translate their product into five languages as a first step into becoming a globally available product. Can you imagine how much more complex that would be if they kept those 14 ways of saying the same thing?

FREQUENCY MAPPING

Frequency mapping is an approach best suited for quantitative data or open questions from surveys. Often referred to as *tag clouds* or *word clouds*, frequency maps represent the repetition of data visually. For open questions from surveys, this technique can represent the frequency of issues (Figure 13-9), while with ranked data it can show the importance of features.

FIGURE 13-9
Sample tag cloud of popular ecommerce search terms

For more information, see *Practical Statistics for Data Scientists* by Peter Bruce and Andrew Bruce (O'Reilly).

SPECTRUM ANALYSIS

Spectrum analysis is the process of looking at the context surfaced by your data points. Rather than organize data points as a collective group, with this approach you refer back to your customer journeys, personas, and workflows and map data points to the point in the process you are looking to study. When you analyze data in this way, opportunities and challenges literally jump out of the page to you. This approach can even be done digitally, through annotated PDFs (Figure 13-10).

For more information on spectrum analysis, see Shlomo Goltz's article "A Closer Look at Personas: A Guide to Developing the Right Ones (Part 2)" (*https://www.smashingmagazine.com/2014/08/a-closer-look-at-personas-part-2*).

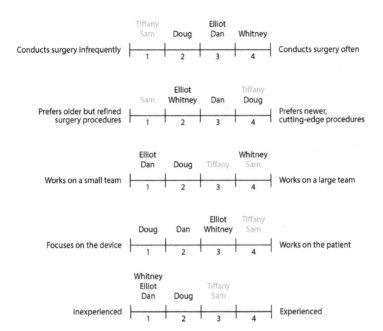

FIGURE 13-10
Sample spectrum analysis placing participants along a behavioral scale

Insights Inform the Design Process

All of these processes of analysis are valuable, but you might be asking, "What does this offer me?" Ultimately, analysis leads to insights, and insights inform the design process.

DESIGN

Think back to the beginning of a new project. You probably felt a bit naïve about the details of that domain. Having completed some research, you now have a greater understanding of what challenges lie ahead. This understanding comes from research analysis, and those data-supported insights you've gathered inform your design decisions. Design direction is easier to discuss and defend with your client when you have data from real users to refer to. This prevents design justifications like "because I like it."

STRATEGY

Ultimately, a business has a strategic plan for success. By asking good questions of your product's functions, you can answer, "Does the product meet our business needs and how?" A business goal to increase revenue threefold, or increase customer retention, is measurable only against analysis from research.

COMMUNICATING INSIGHTS

Informing design and strategy is an important part of research analysis. But how does this all happen? It starts by crafting a story about the research, the goals, and the opportunities. This is how we communicate insights. Our next chapter will focus on this in more detail.

Exercise: Performing a Candyland Analysis

This exercise looks at your organization skills. Rather than working with project data, though, you're going to use candy.

1. **Gather your candy.**

   Rather than purchasing dozens of candy bars, refer to *USA Today's* curated list of the most popular candies (*http://content.usatoday.com/communities/popcandy/post/2011/02/list-the-top-50-candies-of-all-time/1#.V8ZAfpMrLOY*).

2. **Organize the candy.**

   Think about how you can organize the candy in the list. On a whiteboard, sticky notes, or other tool, take 5–10 minutes to organize the candy list.

3. **Pause and reflect.**

   Look back to how you organized the candy. Was it by size? Satisfaction? Flavor (e.g., fruity or chocolatey)? Personal preference?

4. **Change your perspective.**

   Now choose another lens to review the data points from, and take another 5–10 minutes to reorganize the data. How have your insights changed between the first and second round of organization?

Parting Thoughts

Data analysis can often be daunting and time-consuming. This is no reason to shy away from it, though. Some of your best "aha" moments will come after hours of sorting through data. Rather than fight the tedium of analysis, make it a game. Invite your team members, take breaks, and engage in the process in a social and collaborative way. By doing this, you not only invite other perspectives into the analysis but also open yourself up to critique and opportunities to learn from your entire team. Research shouldn't be done alone, and neither should analysis. While analyzing, keep in mind the story you want to tell, as we continue to our next chapter.

[14]

Communicating Insights

The single biggest problem in communication is the illusion that it has taken place.
—GEORGE BERNARD SHAW

You've conducted research and pored over the data to gain insights. But your job isn't done yet: you still need to present those findings to show the value of your research. These steps ensure a user-centered design for your product, and validate the need for further research in the product's lifecycle. In this chapter, we will provide guidance on communicating your findings and various methods for presenting them.

Modes of Presenting

The most common format for reporting research is a meeting with the team and product stakeholders. While overused in many ways, presentations are both familiar and easy to share. Used correctly, presentations tell a powerful story. A common mistake is to create one master presentation that is used for any audience. Because master presentations include everything, they are often generic and long. A better approach is to create at least two separate presentations.

EXECUTIVE SUMMARY

The shorter of the two presentations will be your executive summary, a short, 5–10 slide document highlighting what activities were conducted and what was learned. This brief narrative offers a glimpse into the research effort, showcasing insights and goals. The intent is to be brief and not get lost in process or details. Some practitioners choose to start with the executive summary and use that as a framework for the full report. Others choose to use the full report as the encyclopedia of the project and distill the executive summary from that. There is no wrong method, and we suggest you try both to find your preferred method.

FULL REPORT

Regardless of which report is drafted first, you will want a full report as a companion to the executive summary. This more robust document contains further details about the research. A common table of contents for a full report looks like:

Introductions
Provides context of the research, who was involved, and why research was performed.

Research Highlights
Provides the reader with the key findings from the research, and is often similar to the executive summary.

Methods and Activities
Defines the different methods and activities performed by the team.

Users and Recruitment
Summarizes who participated in the research and how the team recruited them.

Logistics and Scope
Describes the different events and logistics, including travel, technology, and timing.

Research Findings
Details the issues, areas of concern, areas of opportunity, and any metrics that were captured.

Recommendations
Suggests changes for the team to consider or specific changes that have already been mocked up.

Next Steps
Lists follow-up activities the team wants to perform based on the findings. This includes other forms of research and specific design efforts.

Voice from the Streets

Dan Brown, Principal at EightShapes, LLC

How do you approach communicating findings to clients?

In reporting research results, the two most important words are "So what?"

When you're considering what to report, it's tempting to behave like a scientist—present the data as objectively as possible. You want to depict an idealized form of your product's audience, absolute and objective in their representation, free from contaminants like business objectives and technical constraints.

But you're not a scientist: you're a member of a product team. Insights have value when they help you and your teammates make decisions, when they can tell you "so what." Creating an artifact at the tail end of your study may not be necessary if you can translate the findings immediately to design decisions. Perhaps your insights tell you what information to prioritize or strip out. Perhaps your insights help you restructure a flow or choose the right words to describe it.

With the "leaning" of UX, stakeholders increasingly don't expect polished reports. Much of my research is captured in a simple text file—a collection of insights, answers to questions, and recommended changes. These notes form the basis of the discussion with the team, and that discussion constitutes the deliverable.

That conversation epitomizes "so what." Through that conversation we dig into what we observed and talk about why it matters. We look at the original research objectives and ask ourselves what we learned. We talk about possible impacts to the product or the design. This could be as micro as the label on a button or as macro as which features we should prioritize.

Research is the most important tool designers have. Great data yields great insights, and great insights yield novel ideas. Where does great data come from? It starts with great questions—questions about what information helps users achieve their goals and what process aligns best with their mental models. It starts with questions about how they perceive different labels and how they think content should be categorized. Our efforts to seek answers to these questions must be driven by the aim to have a positive impact on the product. Our efforts must yield not only answers to questions, but also an understanding of why they matter.

VIDEO AND AUDIO

The most convincing evidence you can provide on what's working and not working is your users' voices. If you have recordings, producing a highlight reel can be a companion to both the executive summary and the full report. It's hard for stakeholders to argue against your research findings when they watch the feedback directly.

PARTICIPANT QUOTES

If you're unable to record sessions, quotes are equally valuable. Any quotes you use should be anonymous, though it is sometimes helpful to provide context through personas or demographics. This context includes what the participant was doing, or which part of the product they were interacting with when quoted.

RESEARCH ARTIFACTS AND DIAGRAMS

While both the executive summary and full report are formal outputs of research, it is the sum of many individual pieces that allows these stories to be told. The artifacts you use vary based on your method and the audience's interest. For many efforts, you will use a mix of models to represent your findings. As you create new diagrams, try turning them into templates so you have a baseline to work from in future endeavors.

Experience maps

The experience from using products evolves over time. An experience map (Figure 14-1) gives teams perspective and an understanding of different touchpoints and challenges of their users. Stakeholders find value in experience maps' objective representation of their product's impact on the lives of customers.

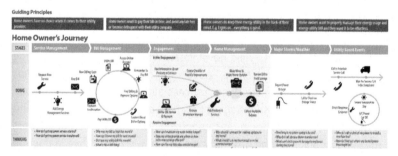

FIGURE 14-1

An experience map illustrating the different touchpoints of a typical home owner

For more information on experience maps, see *Mapping Experiences* by James Kalbach (O'Reilly).

Personas

It can be difficult to recall the different behaviors and qualities of your product's users. A persona (Figure 14-2) captures key points of interest for a user segment and makes it easily digestible for teams and stakeholders.

Lucia | "explorer"

Age: 32 years old
Location: Portland, ME
Hobbies: Running, video games, fly fishing, woodworking

Moment in time: pre-application

"I've been saving for a few years now, and I feel that I'm ready to buy a house. I've done some research on mortgages, but I don't completely understand what is "right" for me given that I am unsure what my credit is. I just want to have official information that will help me make a decision."

About
Lucia is a foreman at a local construction company, but on the side she does a lot of DIY projects to improve her apartment which she shares with her dog, a Belgian Malinois named Max, that her brother gave her for her birthday about 10 years ago. She spends a lot of time searching online for houses and goes to see them to determine if it is a good house to invest in, but she doesn't completely get the different mortgages available to her, though she knows that mortgages are really complex, and she feels ready to dive in and understand it. Lucia wants to find a tool that she can use and trust that will help her get the information that she needs so she can get a mortgage and buy a house.

Needs & wants
- To get a mortgage so she can buy a house
- To find a trustworthy tool to use for her mortgage research
- To understand what is "good/right" when it comes to a mortgage for a person like her
- To understand all of the differences between the different products available for her
- To get the best possible deal in a mortgage

Motivations
- Saving money
- Understanding how to make a good decision
- Making a good decision
- Being knowledgeable enough to negotiate with a broker or a lender
- Having a house of her own

Pain points
- Feeling talked down to
- Difficult to use interfaces
- Too much content, not well organized
- Having to go to multiple places to get one answer
- Not understanding where the information comes from and if it's trustworthy

Behaviors (1-10 scale - scrubbers, please)
Technology/Internet comfort: 9
Mobile apps: 8
Social networks: 7
Researching new information: 8
Asking questions: 9
Self-confidence: 9
Self-questioning: 4
Skepticism: 7

Questions
- How do I know I can trust this?
- How can I tell how much my loan is going to cost?
- How do I know which product is best for me?
- How can I leverage this when I speak to a broker/lender?
- Can I access these tools from my phone?
- How likely am I to get the interest rates displayed?

Goals
To help her shop for different products
To get her to compare different products
To help her understand the different options available for her
To help Lucia make a decision about what is "right" for her

Image source: http://www.dol.gov/_sec/newsletter/2014/20140612-2.htm

FIGURE 14-2
A persona highlighting the behaviors of one key user group as illustrated by this behavioral and demographic data (courtesy of Eduardo Ortiz)

For more information on personas, see *The Persona Lifecycle* by John Pruitt and Tamara Adlin (Elsevier).

Mind maps

As discussed in Chapter 13, every research effort results in piles of data points. A mind map (Figure 14-3) brings those data points together and highlights various connections. You can communicate different viewpoints by visually emphasizing the relevant areas of the map. For more information on mind maps, see *http://www.mindmapping.com*.

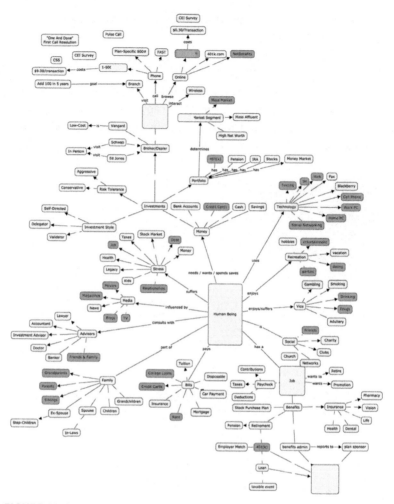

FIGURE 14-3

A mind map capturing connected and related themes about personal finance

User flows

As products become smart and interconnected, workflows become more complex and more challenging to understand. By mapping the overall flow of how a user performs actions, you can avoid unknown pitfalls. A user flow (Figure 14-4) doesn't dictate the final design, but informs the team of key considerations.

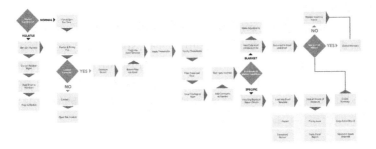

FIGURE 14-4
User flow illustrating interteam workflow and steps

For more information on user flows, see *Interaction Flow Modeling Language* by Marco Brambilla and Piero Fraternali (Elsevier).

Swim lanes

Where user flows map out behaviors of a single user, swim lanes (Figure 14-5) map out triggers and touchpoints across multiple actors, services, or systems. This diagram communicates complexities spanning multiple sources, spaces, or time. The value of swim lanes over user flows is developing an understanding of a variety of aspects of an experience versus a single moment or task.

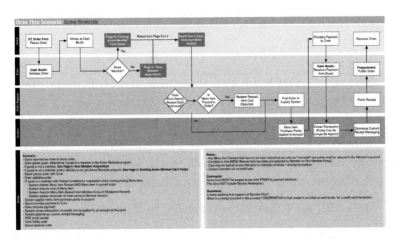

FIGURE 14-5
Swim lanes illustrating the steps and different systems and people involved in a company's rewards program (courtesy of Russ Unger)

For more information on creating swim lanes, see *https://leancor.com/blog/how-to-create-a-swim-lane-diagram*.

Mental models

Research offers a lens into another's perspective that allows teams to create detailed mental models (Figure 14-6), sometimes spanning the length of a conference room. These diagrams provide inventories of thoughts and actions users make in a defined context. The insights gained inform how a product supports or hinders the user's goals and needs.

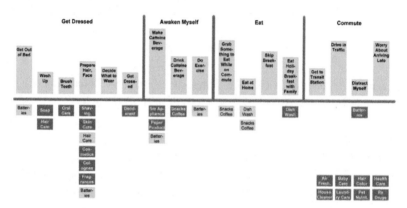

FIGURE 14-6

A user's mental model of their morning routine

For more information, see *Mental Models* by Indi Young (Rosenfeld Media).

Severity scales

The volume of issues resulting from testing can slow down progress. To focus teams and prioritize, label each issue with a severity rating. These ratings inform the timeline for future fixes.

A common severity scale teams use is the Nielsen Norman Group's Severity Ratings for Usability Problems (*https://www.nngroup.com/articles/how-to-rate-the-severity-of-usability-problems*):

0 = I don't agree that this is a usability problem at all.

1 = Cosmetic problem only; need not be fixed unless extra time is available on project.

2 = Minor usability problem; fixing this should be given low priority.

3 = Major usability problem; important to fix, so should be given high priority.

4 = Usability catastrophe; imperative to fix this before product can be released.

Click maps

Where people click on a screen tells you a lot about what they're interested in and how well the information hierarchy works. In conjunction with or in place of eye tracking, click maps (Figure 14-7) illustrate the journey a user took within your system.

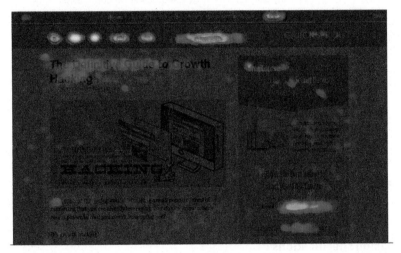

FIGURE 14-7
Click map illustrating areas of focus on a web page

Actionable recommendations

Nobody likes to be told what's wrong without being offered a solution. One of the most valuable things you can do is offer recommendations to your team and stakeholders on what could come next. Even if these guidelines are incomplete, they provide a starting point for future iteration and storytelling.

Change logs

Design is fast paced, and design iterations happen quicker than new releases. By keeping a change log associated with different research artifacts, product teams can track versions and see how feedback evolves—hopefully becoming more positive—over time (see Figure 14-8).

Change Log

DATE	VERSION	AUTHOR	CHANGE DESCRIPTION
6-13	1	Nathan Stark	First draft
6-14	1.1	Tony Banner	Revised based on comments from Carol Jones
6-15	1.2	Steve Barton	Refining further
6-16	1.3	Tony Banner	Revised based on comments from Natasha Stacy
6-16	1.4	Steve Barton	Revised based on comments from Natasha Stacy
6-16	1.5	Nathan Stark	Revised based on comments from Carol Jones and Aven Team

FIGURE 14-8
Sample change log for product documentation

Design specifications

Not all teams are colocated, which makes communicating details risky to overall quality. Design specs are documents that communicate the expected interactions and any constraints to the product team (see Figure 14-9). They support research teams in focusing on the features and scope immediately impacting business goals.

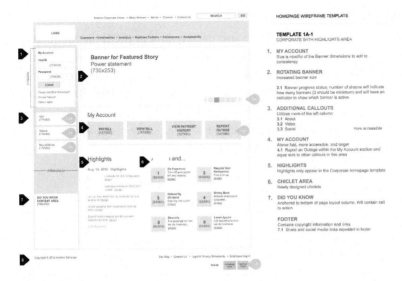

FIGURE 14-9

A sample page from a design spec illustrating annotated wireframes

Importance of Different Modes

Research allows teams to reevaluate their assumptions about a product and motivates conversations, bringing new life to your strategy. The story you craft offers the opportunity to share learning and lessons in an actionable way.

REPORTING

Most forms of user experience research can be expensive. It can take weeks, if not months, to conduct and analyze research. During that time, design and development efforts might slow down or be on hold. You have to account for the expenses associated with research. Typical research could cost thousands of dollars, even for simple studies. While this might seem steep, the risk of not conducting research is a poor or ineffective product. To justify costs, use findings reports to inform stakeholders of the tangible, financial impact your research provides. These reports serve as historical records of how a product was developed.

MAKING THE ROI CASE

Research reports show the return on investment (ROI) for conducting research. Reports may illustrate that initial assumptions were wrong, which led to lost time and money spent developing the wrong product. By using quantitative findings, you can refine overall product strategy with the support of hard data. Qualitative validation of changes the team makes will highlight higher revenue, lower costs, and improvements to the customer experience.

USING DIFFERENT FORMS OF STORYTELLING

The medium of research reports differs based on the stage of your product development, the method of research, and the audience. For example, for high-profile executives you will want to go over the executive summary so they can quickly hear what activities were performed and why they matter. With your team, you'll want something more detailed and tied directly to the day-to-day work they do.

Using the Artifacts

The artifacts you create can be used to inform your team's current work as well as product strategy. These documents become part of the team's toolset and should be referenced often, not simply lost in an archive folder.

TEAM USE

Research findings have both near- and long-term benefits to your team. The findings inform immediate design decisions and set the team up to create a better product strategy.

Capture immediate value with actionable tasks

Each insight should be distilled into actionable tasks that can be added to your product backlog. Tasks should reference the research artifacts to provide rationale and context for the request.

When presenting new work based on research, explain why the solution benefits the customer and reiterate the research findings. This helps to frame critique and eventually leads to a higher-quality solution.

Project long-term value with product roadmaps

A common question you'll hear when delivering findings is "What now? What will you look at next?" As mentioned previously, you often have more questions after research than at the beginning. Share these questions with your stakeholders in the form of future areas of inquiry. There is no time like the present to ask for both permission and funding to start your next round of research.

One way to show how research data can be used for long-term value is creating a product roadmap (Figure 14-10). A product roadmap outlines the areas of focus for the team over the next few months. Include future research efforts you want to pursue, illustrating how they line up with your product development efforts.

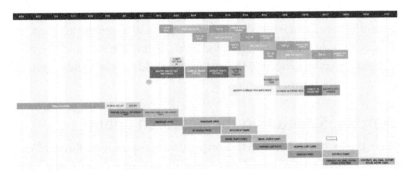

FIGURE 14-10
Product roadmap highlighting the overlap of design and research over the course of a product lifecycle

STAKEHOLDER USE

Research findings are just as invaluable to business stakeholders as to the product team. While the motivations behind the findings differ, there are a few key ways to address business needs.

Include stakeholder observations

For stakeholders who observed sessions, capture their comments. Although it's biased, the stakeholder's point of view is important to capture. By pointing to a stakeholder and saying, "Remember when you saw the user struggle with feature X?" you build allies and reinforce that data is leading product development. These same quotes can help you counter uninformed comments from stakeholders who didn't observe research. For instance, if the vice president hears from her trusted field manager that a core feature of a product didn't work, she is more likely to believe it and want to correct the issue than if she hears it from you

Integrate stakeholder interests and opinions

When planning the findings report, structure and highlight areas based on what you know about your audience. Balance the stakeholder observations and quick wins with bigger challenges and discoveries from the data.

Remove yourself

Research data is more credible when your own biases are removed. Balance this with your experience and turn observations into actionable insights. This raises the quality of your findings and makes it more difficult for stakeholders to argue against recommendations. If stakeholders do refute a recommendation, refer to the data and the specific participants. Chapter 13 illustrates methods to code and organize data points for future reference.

Exercise: Structuring the Research Report

There is a lot of information that goes into a research report, regardless of the research method used. Starting with the report's structure, outlined here, ensures that it is accepted and easy to use.

1. **Define why this matters.**

   Think of a current project you've conducted or are planning to conduct research on. Write down what you want to communicate and define the audience. These statements should answer why your audience should care about your report, what insights were gained, and why the project matters in the first place.

2. **Write down your content inventory.**

   Write down on sticky notes or note cards all the content you could include in the report. Be as broad as possible, including written, visual, and audio components.

3. **Card-sort the content.**

   Sort the content types and group them, similar to an affinity diagram. Don't worry about naming clusters until the initial sorting is completed. Note any outliers and, unless you're offering earth-shattering insights, don't include them in your report. Craft a label that represents each cluster. These labels become section headers for your report.

4. **Reduce the content.**

   Review each cluster and determine what content types don't carry enough weight to be included in the report. These can be pieces of content that don't have enough evidence to defend, or that represent something the team is already aware of and don't bear repeating.

5. **Write the report.**

   Determine the best medium for your report and start writing. Use the clusters to guide you and to locate supporting evidence that will create a solid research report.

Parting Thoughts

For many researchers, the research report is the only evidence of the time, money, and effort they've spent on research. For business stake-holders, you want to ensure that challenges and objections are pre-sented, validated, and discussed in an informed manner. For your project team, you want to ensure anyone can reference the document a week, a month, or years later and have sufficient context to make informed decisions. While product strategy and cycles are ever chang-ing, a well-constructed research report offers insights into both known and unknown challenges and into what mistakes can be avoided. Over time, you will find research is an ongoing activity, either formally or informally, and the ability to casually refer back to older documents is invaluable in this process.

[15]

Getting the Most Out of Research

Study the past if you would define the future.
—CONFUCIUS

Every research effort can be used to springboard a new phase of understanding about your users and your product. Teams often feel a desire to continue research initiatives after observing the positive impact from a single study. In this final chapter, we leave you with some advice on how to continue conducting research and recap a few of the key concepts covered in the book.

Research Starts with Questions

Every team wonders what their product should do and what they think people do with their product. These questions lead teams down the path of research. As questions are answered, new questions surface that weren't expected. Research is a process that enables team knowledge to grow and mature over time, which results in an excellent product both for the business and its users.

WHAT DO WE THINK WE KNOW?

Knowledge doesn't cause problems. Lack of knowledge does. Identifying what is known and, more importantly, what is unknown allows for continual improvement and keeps users engaged. One model you can use to understand a product's use is a *conscious competency matrix*. This model communicates the level of knowledge or understanding for a team or individual, and where that team or individual has room to grow. This matrix may be defined in the four quadrants, as outlined in Figure 15-1.

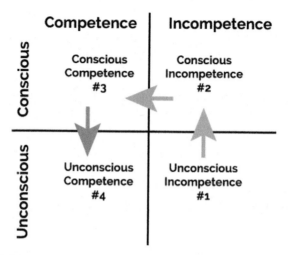

FIGURE 15-1

The conscious competency matrix illustrates the transition between knowledge phases across four main phases

Unconsciously incompetent

At the start of a project, you won't know what challenges exist around a product space. You know research needs to happen, but are unsure what specific questions or opportunities exist.

Consciously incompetent

Your team begins to understand what questions might be asked and whom the target audience is. They are able to identify what information is missing and why it is of value.

Consciously competent

You understand user behavior and how and in what contexts your product is used. You actively draw on this knowledge to build a roadmap of improvements the team can make.

Unconsciously competent

You can now apply your understanding of the user and product to other areas of the organization or inspire new products to be developed. You should look for new areas of inquiry to fuel new research so the overall pool of knowledge can continue to grow.

As more and more research is conducted, your team can track their level of understanding across this matrix to keep themselves honest and remove their biases. The goal should be to reach the unconscious competence zone. At the same time, your team will understand what product-related areas still need additional investigation and discovery.

As you continue to conduct research, you will see your skills and comfort level with different approaches shift too. You will outgrow this book and move on to more specific and targeted pieces of literature that can strengthen specific research muscles.

WHAT DO WE WANT TO KNOW?

Good product teams know research never stops. Research isn't always in-depth or time-consuming, but should continue throughout a product development's lifecycle. Common areas of ongoing research include:

- Validation of recent changes
- Experimentation with microcontent and design patterns
- Common pitfalls and drop-off points
- Overall user satisfaction

Research Is Ongoing

There will always be areas you want to learn about, new and old. User behavior changes over time, due to life events or the natural progression of technology. How these changes impact your product should be an area of focus for you and your team.

PLAN YOUR NEXT EFFORTS

Internal workshops move teams up on the competency matrix because they get current information and understanding out in the open. The resulting conversations inform which research methods could be employed next. Regardless of whether you're doing quantitative or qualitative research, you have a captive audience ready to provide the desired information.

Voice from the Streets

Ofer Deshe, CEO, Tobias & Tobias

How does research impact your work and approach to product design?

Research is the real key to game-changing growth in today's disrupted world.

It's an uncertain world for CEOs. Most industries are facing unprecedented disruption from challenger brands and new entrants. Smart systems and digital tools are fundamentally changing how we work, the products we create, and how we sell them. In this competitive landscape changes are rapid, choice is in abundance, and the bargaining powers of buyers are on the rise. Sustainable growth requires customers that adopt your services, engage with you more deeply, and value you enough to become—and remain—loyal.

Most firms are good at understanding and designing their own architectures, operating frameworks, structures, policies, procedures, and technologies. But the real key to unlocking game-changing opportunities for growth is to deeply understand the people you are looking to serve. Deep understanding of your customers' cognitive, emotional, and behavioral characteristics cannot come from analytics and market research alone. The former shows what people are already doing and the latter captures their attitudes, but both are poor predictors of the likely success of a future proposition.

Investment in innovation is often significant and risky, so adopting the right customer research approaches is essential. As a CEO, I prefer to rely on structured observations, ethnographic studies, and methods rooted in sociology and psychology. Many of these techniques have already made their way into the arsenal of tools used by some of the world's most innovative firms. The right research uncovers new insights about customers' unmet needs and validates hypotheses and assumptions. This understanding can unlock innovation opportunities and help shape propositions that customers will perceive as valuable and love. Too often, I encounter leadership teams that dream up product ideas in brainstorming sessions, boardrooms, and off-site hotels. By failing to integrate structured research into their product development lifecycle, these firms test the desirability of new propositions when it is far too late.

Put simply, to truly differentiate, one must move from a technology-focused paradigm of launching minimally viable products and seeing what might happen, to an evidence-based and customer-centric world of minimally lovable services. Good research is great for business and provides a high return on investment. Bad or no research reduces revenues and profitability and, ultimately, contributes to brand failure.

DIVE DEEPER

It's rare to gain a complete understanding about how people behave, because eventually the team needs to work on building the product. Research data gets stale over time, and findings from two years ago may no longer apply to what the team is working on today. Take this opportunity to revisit topics that you and the team felt were "fully understood" and ask new questions to gain a deeper understanding.

If you used only qualitative methods to dive into your users' worlds, find quantitative methods that provide a new point of view—and vice versa. There is always another stone to turn over and new data points to dig up that can give the team the information they need to have their next breakthrough.

RESEARCH IS INTEGRATED

The wonderful thing about research is that it can be applied to so many different areas of an organization and a product's lifecycle. Even when focused on one aspect of a product, research offers insights that could have a wide impact on your team's product.

Product development

Product teams exist to develop products, and research based on actual user behavior leads to more successful solutions. Rather than let your assumptions and personal opinions sway a design, remember that nothing beats observable truths.

For more information, see Steven Hoober's article "The Role of User Experience in the Product Development Process" (*http://www.uxmatters .com/mt/archives/2014/05/the-role-of-user-experience-in-the-product -development-process.php*).

Product roadmap

Findings from research remind your team to look at the whole picture. When you're focused on the day-to-day development of the product, it's hard to think about how that product could evolve. The information captured from research guides the team into thinking about the backlog and helps them prioritize.

For more information, see Frank Guo's article "Leveraging UX Insights to Influence Product Strategy" (*http://www.uxmatters.com/mt/ archives/2011/09/leveraging-ux-insights-to-influence-product-strategy. php*).

Business strategy

The way consumers purchase, subscribe, and interact with products changes almost every few years. Research insights inform your interactions with customers, marketing strategy, and tactics to draw new customers.

For more information, see Robert Fabricant's article "The Rise of UX Leadership" (*https://hbr.org/2013/07/the-rise-of-ux-leadership*).

Team culture

The whole product team benefits from engaging with users, through qualitative and quantitative methods. It allows the team to become closer to the people they are working for and to rethink how they are approaching their product development. By having an empathic link to the users thanks to the information gleaned from research, teams are more likely to make decisions that better support user goals and needs.

For more information, see Jeffrey Easton's article "Five Strategies for Moving Your Company Toward User Centricity" (*http://www. humanfactors.com/newsletters/five-strategies-for-moving-your-company-toward-user-centricity.asp*).

RESEARCH IS A LIFESTYLE

Your research skills and techniques will always be changing and growing. As you practice a variety of approaches, your ability to identify areas that deserve research will improve. Research is an addictive process for many teams and often becomes a core component of product team's culture.

Increasing nimbleness

By incorporating research into every facet of your product develop-ment, you and the team can quickly adapt to changes that happen. You never know when a new competitor will enter the marketplace, or when new devices become available that alter user interactions with technol-ogy. Referring back to the competency matrix, this is the sweet spot of being unconsciously competent. Once there, you and your team know enough to be able to make educated decisions about the development of your product, and will realize when you're approaching unknown territory.

Parting Thoughts

We hope you've enjoyed this book and have taken something from it. As you perform research, remember it is a journey into the unknown. It is exciting, daunting, and highly addictive. The result is a set of skills that's akin to a superpower.

The ability to identify real problems quicker and more efficiently increases your value to your team and product alike. Ultimately, what started as a singular research initiative turns into a thirst to speak with users, collaborate with stakeholders, and iterate with tangible data and not assumptions.

Embrace the thrill of discovery, exploration, and execution. Most impor-tantly, remember to have fun.

[*Index*]

Slide Show improv game, 141–142
small talk, 128–130
smartphone usage, 34
socialization stage (cyborg anthropology), 11–12
soft skills in facilitators
about, 151–153
microexpressions, 159–162
reading body language, 153–159
Soucy, Kyle, 158–159
spectrum analysis, 194–195
spreadsheets for tracking data, 172, 188–189
stakeholders
communicating with, 168–170, 199–210
determining goals of, 67–68
interviewing, 60–61, 71, 193
participatory design and, 58
using artifacts, 211–212
workshops for, 59
Strawbridge, Ron, 80–81
strengths (SWOT analysis), 192
structure of questions, 23–24
student role, 113
supplies list, 77
surprise (facial expression), 161
SurveyMonkey, 39
surveys
about, 38–39, 43, 59
choosing methods and, 67, 194
as recruitment screeners, 96
Survs tool, 39
swim lanes, 205–206
SWOT analysis, 192
system analytics, 37–38, 43–44, 67

T

tag clouds, 194
tasks, actionable, 210
taxonomy
in qualitative reviews, 59
in quantitative reviews, 37, 39–40, 43
library sciences and, 15
teacher role, 113
team members
communicating with, 171, 167–168
ongoing research and, 217–221
team culture and, 220

using artifacts, 210–211
welcome kit information
about, 81
technology
digital affinity diagrams, 173–174
improvisation and, 147
remote challenges, 79–80, 170
tech checks, 76–77
testing
feedback from, 171
hypotheses, 168
in qualitative research, 57, 60
in quantitative research, 35–37, 41
usability, 60, 80, 158
The Persona Lifecycle (Pruitt and Adlin), 203
thermostats, 8–9, 35
think-aloud studies, 55–56
threats (SWOT analysis), 192
time-based questions, 27–28
timeline and research approach, 69
Toastmasters, 133–134
Tobias & Tobias, 218
Tobii eye-tracking software, 40–41
Toyota, 5
tracking data
affinity diagrams for, 172–174, 190–191
highlight reels, 174–175, 202
importance of, 171–172
spreadsheets for, 172, 188–189
training participants, 80
travel considerations, 78–79
tree jacking, 39–40, 43, 69
Treejack tool, 40, 42
Trello tool, 173
Tufte, Edward, 33

U

unconsciously competent phase, 216
unconsciously incompetent phase, 216
Unger, Russ, 205
University of Chicago, 4
unmoderated product testing/validation, 43, 57–59
usability testing, 60, 80, 158
user flows, 204
user profiles, 92–94
User Testing tool, 57–58

[*About the Authors*]

Brad Nunnally is a User Experience Designer out of St. Louis, MO. He regularly speaks on research methods, design techniques, and strategy. For the last decade, his work has included research, modeling, design, and testing. Over the course of his career, he has helped clients in the financial, healthcare management, public utilities, and pharmaceutical management industries identify user needs and develop engaging experiences based on those needs.

David Farkas is a User Experience Designer in Philadelphia, PA. David started his career in-house, has worked in consultancies of all sizes, has had opportunities to craft the design process within an organization, and has also adopted and evolved existing paradigms. His experience includes a range of financial services systems, business systems, and ecommerce and cross-channel platforms.